By the
Bathroom Readers'
Institute

Bathroom Readers' Press
Ashland, Oregon

UNCLE JOHN'S BATHROOM READER® FOR GIRLS ONLY!

Cover design: Dorit Ely
Photo credit, page 182: Yves Picq

For information, write:
The Bathroom Readers' Institute, P.O. Box 1117,
Ashland, OR 97520
www.bathroomreader.com • 888-488-4642

ISBN-13: 978-1-60710-179-6 / ISBN-10: 1-60710-179-3

Library of Congress Cataloging-in-Publication Data
Uncle John's bathroom reader for girls only.
p. cm.
ISBN 978-1-60710-179-6 (pbk.)
1. Women—Miscellanea. 2. Curiosities and wonders.
3. American wit and humor. I. Bathroom Readers' Institute
(Ashland, Or.) II. Title.
PN6338.W6U53 2011
081.02'07—dc22

2010044901

Printed in Crawfordsville, Indiana,
United States of America

First Printing

1 2 3 4 5 15 14 13 12 11

THANK YOU

The Bathroom Readers' Institute sincerely thanks the people whose advice and assistance made this book possible.

Gordon Javna
Amy Miller
Jahnna Beecham
Malcolm Hillgartner
Maggie McLaughlin
Dorit Ely
Jay Newman
Brian Boone
Kim Griswell
Melinda Allman
Dan Mansfield
Michael Conover
Eleanor Pierce
Jessika Shannon
Marie Mathay
Michael Kerr

Rob Proctor
Skye McKenna
Lindsay Galt
Angela Kern
Claudia Bauer
JoAnn Padgett
Monica Maestas
Amy Ly & Annie Lam
Sydney Stanley
Ginger Winters
David Calder
Erin Corbin
Tom Mustard
Publishers Group West
Caesar & Deja
Thomas Crapper

TABLE OF CONTENTS

Because the BRI understands your reading needs, we've divided the contents by length as well as subject.

Short—a quick read

Medium—2 pages

Long—3 to 5 pages (that's not too long, is it?)

ADVENTURE CALLS

LIFE IS STRANGE

X-TREME WOMEN

FUN & GAMES

INTRODUCTION

One day we were sitting around at the BRI, trying to think of an idea for our next book, when—amid all the pencil-tapping, potato-chip-crunching, and other deep-thinking sounds—somebody finally said, "I know! Let's do a *Bathroom Reader* just for girls!" It was a great idea, so the rest of us started scribbling down lists of topics that girls might be interested in. But then the lists got longer…and longer…and longer. Why? Because we realized that girls are interested in *everything*.

So that's what we made: *Uncle John's Bathroom Reader for Girls Only*—a book about everything.

Here's just a sampling of what you'll find inside:

• A girl who picked up a ukulele and started an internet sensation (page 85).

• A woman who walked across Europe…twice (page 211).

• An Australian who blogs about her mysterious life as a geisha (page 234).

• Jane Goodall (page 189), Rihanna (page 252), and Emily Dickinson (page 151).

• And if you've ever wondered whether Natalie Portman did her own dancing in *Black Swan* (page 137), how to make a cupcake in a coffee mug (page 176), or how much water Katy Perry drinks (page 25), it's all in here.

This book didn't write itself (though there's probably an app for that), so we'd like to send out a hearty thank-you to our own Jahnna, who penned most of what you'll read here. We'd also like to thank the crack team who helped her: researcher *extraordinaire* Maggie, story wrangler Malcolm, traffic cop Amy, super-writers Marie, Rob, Eleanor, Jessika, and the two Michaels. And a special shout-out to artist Dorit, who wore out a few (electronic) paintbrushes to give us a beautiful cover.

We think you'll find this book as much fun to read as it was to write. And if you do, let us know! Fan us on Facebook, tweet us on Twitter, and wave at our website. Or even better, tell us what you'd like to see in the next *Bathroom Reader for Girls Only*. With a whole world of girls out there, we know there's plenty more to write about. So happy reading.

And as always,

Go With the Flow!

Uncle John
and the BRI Staff

CAUTION: PARENTS TEXTING

Sometimes parents like to show they're cool while texting. But judging by these real texts that kids posted on the internet, they don't always succeed.

Mom: Hi, have a good day. Love mum.

Me: Mum! You learned how to text??

Mom: Hi, have a good day. Love mum.

Me: Can you type anything besides that?

Mom: Hi, have a good day. Love mum.

Dad: We have a lot of phone numbers:)

Me: Dad…Stop using so many smileys

Dad: I only use them with you.

Me: Still weird.

Dad: :'(

Dad: The key is under the cat.

Me: I hope you meant mat.

Dad: ytesd

Dad: wat u doing

Me: About to shower. You?

Dad: Peeing

Mom: Hey! Check out the birthday greeting I put up on your brother's FB!

Me: It just says, "Happy birthday!"

Mom: Yeah. I thought it would be nice.

Dad: are you doing your math

Me: really daddy? from the basement? ye of little faith…

Dad: I notice you did not say yes

Grandpa: I love you!

Me: I love you too! You're the best!

Grandpa: At what?

In 2008 Russia tried—and failed—to pass a law forbidding teenagers to wear "goth" clothing.

WHAT'S MY FIRST LINE?

Can you match each famous first line with its famous book?

1. "When Mary Lennox was sent to Misselthwaite Manor to live with her uncle, everybody said she was the most disagreeable child ever seen. It was true, too."
2. "These two very old people are the father and mother of Mr. Bucket."
3. "It was a dark and stormy night."
4. "Mr. and Mrs. Dursley of number four, Privet Drive, were proud to say that they were perfectly normal, thank you very much."
5. "Once there were four children whose names were Peter, Susan, Edmund, and Lucy."
6. "It is a truth universally acknowledged, that a single man in possession of a good fortune must be in want of a wife."
7. "When he was nearly thirteen, my brother Jem got his arm badly broken at the elbow."
8. "'Where's Papa going with that axe?' said Fern to her mother as they were setting the table for breakfast."

a. *The Lion, the Witch and the Wardrobe*
b. *To Kill a Mockingbird*
c. *Pride and Prejudice*
d. *The Secret Garden*
e. *Charlie and the Chocolate Factory*
f. *Harry Potter and the Sorcerer's Stone*
g. *Charlotte's Web*
h. *A Wrinkle in Time*

ANSWERS: 1–d; 2–e; 3–h; 4–f; 5–a; 6–c; 7–b; 8–g.

GIRL GAMERS

About 40 percent of all video-game players are female, but relatively few women work in the video-game industry. Still, even in this male-dominated business, some women have found their dream jobs—by honing their gaming skills from an early age. Result: Now they get paid to play video games!

HEX MARKS HER SPOT

Stephanie "Hex" Bendixsen's parents never allowed her to have a game console at home, so she would sneak to a friend's house to play *SimCity*... and she was hooked. After she finished high school in Australia, she condensed a whole childhood's worth of gaming into a few years. Now, at 25, she's the host of *Good Game*, an Australian television program where she rates games, interviews developers, tells the latest gaming news, and offers game tips. What's her advice for girls looking to make video games into a career? "I think girls just need to be more vocal about being geeky and being into games."

YOUR LIFE MIGHT CHANGE OVERNIGHT

After college, Lucy Song started looking for a job, but the search was difficult and tiring. She played video games to relieve the stress, and that got her thinking about designing her own game. She started working on it, and day by day, she added to her pet project. She

World's first human cannonball: a 14-year-old girl named Zazel, of the London Circus (1877).

mentioned it at a party, and a friend told her about a video-game company that was hiring new employees. In less than a year, Song became a community manager, moderating a discussion forum and writing articles for game developer ChangYou. Here's what she learned about landing your dream job: "Never miss a chance to show your enthusiasm, because you never know who might be listening. And never give up. Even if you fail again and again, you never know how much your life might change overnight."

"I GET TO BE A BIG KID!"

Sally Reynolds is a quality-assurance technician for the British video-game company Jagex. In other words, her job is to play video games. Really. Sally worked her way into her dream job by starting with an entry-level position at Jagex. Then, when the company began looking for a game tester, she asked for the job. "I make sure the games are bug-free and ready for release," she says. "I get to do what I like doing for fun. I love my job. I get to be a big kid!"

BEAT IT WITH BROOKELYN

Brooke Hattabaugh is a hard-core gamer. How hard-core? A boyfriend once broke up with her because she spent too much time playing. But it's more than just her hobby; it's her career. She works for video-game maker Ubisoft as part of an all-female group of professional gamers called the Frag Dolls. Hattabaugh, who goes by the game name "Brookelyn," travels the United States promoting new games and encouraging other girls to play them. She got her job through an online want ad. "I didn't think it was a real ad," she said. "I didn't even send in a real résumé, I sent a gamer résumé with the names of all the games I had played and beaten." It worked.

DREAM FOR A LIVING

Amy Kalson was a computer programmer, but that was just to pay the bills—her real passion was writing. In 2000 she went to California as a freelance journalist to write a story about a video-game conference. There she caught a glimpse of the game *Final Fantasy VIII*, and it changed her life. "It mesmerized me," Kalson says. Soon she discovered that video games blended all of her favorite interests: storytelling, technology, theater, music, myth, and history. She also noticed that there were very few games designed for women. (Even today, 9 out of 10 game programmers are male.) So she enrolled at Carnegie Mellon University to study entertainment technology, and by the time she graduated she had already worked on *The Sims 2* and *The Sims Unleashed*. Today she is a senior design producer at Disney Interactive. What does she do all day? "I travel around the country, meeting with all kinds of developers who are making games for Disney. I brainstorm game ideas and come up with the heart and soul of new games. And I get to dream for a living."

What are *blindsies*, *hopsies*, and *yokeys*? Jump-rope tricks.

"T" IS FOR *TWILIGHT*

Ever hear of beginner's luck? Well, first-time author Stephenie Meyer had loads of it.

OUT OF THE ORDINARY

In early 2003, Stephenie Meyer was like a lot of American women: a stay-at-home mom taking care of her three little boys, Gabe, Seth, and Eli. She'd never written anything in her life, not even a short story, and the only professional job she'd ever had was as a receptionist at a property company in Phoenix, Arizona. Her husband was the breadwinner. But that all changed on the night of June 2, 2003, when Meyer had a dream about a human girl and a vampire who was in love with her…but thirsted for her blood.

NIGHTTIME IS THE WRITE TIME

The next day, Meyer sat down and wrote what turned out to be the 13th chapter in the hit book *Twilight*. It took her three months to finish the book, writing whenever she could during the day and after the kids were in bed. Then, with her older sister's encouragement, she sent the manuscript to more than a dozen literary agents. Nine rejected her and five ignored her. But one, Jodi Reamer, accepted the book. By November, only six months after Meyers's vampire dream, her agent sold *Twilight* to the publisher Little, Brown and Company. Meyer fantasized about being paid $10,000 for her book—enough to buy a new van. But her agent and the publisher knew *Twilight* had the potential to be a huge hit…and they signed a three-book deal for a stunning $750,000! *Twilight* was published in 2005 and skyrocketed to #1 on the *New York Times* best-seller list for children's chapter books.

SHINING STAR

Meyer, who used to write with a toddler on her lap watching *Blue's Clues*, is now a full-time author earning more than $50 million per year. Her husband manages the household and takes care of the kids at their home in Cave Creek, Arizona. She's finished the *Twilight* saga and has moved on to other projects, including a science-fiction book and movie, *The Host.* But don't expect her work to be filled with anything R-rated. Meyer was raised a Mormon and, even though she writes about vampires and invasive aliens, she says she's still pretty straitlaced about her beliefs. Her faith, stage plays, music, and classic novels are all sources of inspiration; in fact, Jane Austen, William Shakespeare, and Emily Brontë are the authors whose works influenced her as she wrote about the super-hot romance between Bella and Edward in *Twilight*.

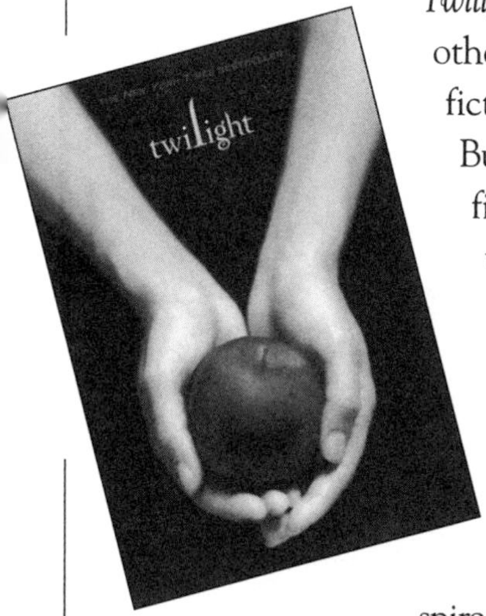

…*Forks*, after the town in Washington where the story is set.

WILL SUCCESS SPOIL STEPHENIE MEYER?

Meyer admits to feeling a little guilty about her instant success. "People [authors] go through so much, and I skipped over the bad parts. It feels like cheating, somehow." But this self-described "girlie girl" is more than grateful to be living the dream.

WHAT'S ON STEPHENIE MEYER'S *TWILIGHT* PLAYLIST?

Meyer confesses, "I can't write without music." Check out what she listened to while she wrote her very first book. (It follows *Twilight*, chapter by chapter.)

1. "Why Does It Always Rain on Me?" Travis
2. "Creep" (radio edit), Radiohead
3. "In My Place," Coldplay
4. "I'm Not Okay (I Promise)" (video edit), My Chemical Romance
5. "With You" (reanimation remix), Linkin Park
6. "By Myself," Linkin Park
7. "Dreaming," OMD
8. "Please Forgive Me," David Gray
9. "Here with Me," Dido
10. "Time Is Running Out," Muse
11. "Tremble for My Beloved," Collective Soul
12. "Dreams," The Cranberries
13. "Lullabye (Goodnight, My Angel)," Billy Joel

***Twilight: New Moon* earned $72.7 million in a single day, the highest one-day box-office sales ever.**

GET ME OUT OF HERE!

If you've ever had to give a speech in class or sing a solo in choir, you've probably felt the butterflies of stage fright. But seasoned actors and musicians never have that problem, right? Wrong.

"I get so terrified before I go onstage. My secret is no eye contact. I find that if I don't look directly at people and just concentrate completely on the singing and dance moves, then I can get through."

—Beyoncé

"I can't ever do theater because I would pee my pants. It's way too nerve-wracking. There's a comfort in being able to mess up when you're on a movie set."

—Emma Roberts

"My stage fright gets worse and worse as I get older. After 40 years you'd think that I'd get over it, but there is no trick to help."

—Ozzy Osbourne

"I definitely get stage fright. That's part of the fun. That's what makes it interesting."

—Zac Efron

"I nearly gave up the Beatles in the early '60s. I remember being on the steps of Wembley Town Hall, literally getting ill with nerves, and thinking, 'I've got to give this business up, this is no good.'"

—Paul McCartney

"Once, somebody told me to picture the audience in their underpants. Do *not* picture the audience in their underpants. That does not work. At all."

—Taylor Swift

"I have moments where I feel invincible and know that I have the audience in my hand—everything is perfect. And then I have panic attacks and I feel everyone is breathing my air and I can't live up to everybody's expectations and I might just die onstage."

—Madonna

BIG MOUTH

Some people have weird talents, like being able to roll their tongue into a funnel or bend their thumb back to touch their wrist. Here's a girl who took her "special skill" a little too far.

OPEN WIDE

Sue S., a teenager in Colorado, had a rare talent: She could put her whole fist in her mouth. (Go ahead—try it.) This amazed her friends so much that they were constantly bringing her things to stick in her mouth. One day, a friend gave her the ultimate challenge: Could she get her mouth around the big doorknob on the science lab's door? Sue bet $10 that she could—and knelt down by the door and did it! The trouble was, once she got her jaw locked around the knob, she couldn't spit it out. To make matters worse, class was in session in the lab, and any second the bell was going to ring and someone would throw open the door and knock her teeth out. While the school nurse ran to call 911, someone else told the science class to leave the room by climbing out the first-floor window. Meanwhile, Sue was stuck—gagging, drooling, and starting to panic, and students were starting to gather, staring and saying things like, "That's the stupidest thing I've ever seen." When the fire-department crew arrived, they had to take the door off its hinges (with Sue still attached) and lay it flat on the floor. They gave Sue a shot in the butt to relax her muscles and, finally, her jaw unlocked. The good news: Sue won the $10.

GODDESSES RULE: PELE

Here's one goddess you don't want to cross. She'll heat your house one day...and burn it down the next.

TEMPER, TEMPER!

According to Hawaiian legend, the explosive goddess of fire known as Pele lives inside the Kilauea volcano on the Big Island of Hawaii. From deep inside the rim, she rules over her feisty family of fire gods. Pele has the power to destroy and create, and her anger erupts in streaming flows of red-hot lava that can engulf humans and animals, turning them to stone. With one stomp of her foot, she can unleash a bone-shaking earthquake. But when Pele is happy and content, she stops any lava from reaching Hawaii's villages and keeps her gentle fires burning so the locals can heat their homes and cook their food. Every now and then, Pele has been known to assume the shape of a woman walking a white dog, and people who have spotted her (and survived) claim she is the most beautiful woman they've ever seen. Not surprisingly, most Pele sightings occur near volcanic craters.

PELE'S CURSE

Pele remains a popular figure in Hawaiian culture today. One superstition says that if you take lava rock, or even a handful of sand, away from Hawaii, Pele will curse you and bad luck will follow. But if you happen to have a piece of souvenir lava sitting around your house and you've had a mysterious run of misfortune, don't despair—

Hawaiian saying: "Take only the flowers and leis you are given, and leave only with aloha."

you can mail your rocks back to the visitors' center at Volcanoes National Park, and the rangers will toss them onto a pile of lava behind the building. If you want to give them a more elaborate "return," Lava-Rock-Return, a service offered by the Volcano Gallery on the Big Island of Hawaii, will bring them back to nature for you…for a small fee. A person named Rainbow Moon wraps your rock in the leaf of a ti plant, a Hawaiian plant that's supposed to bring good luck, and then drops it with an offering of orchids close to the volcano home of Pele.

RETURN TO SENDER

Here are some notes that Lava-Rock-Return and Volcanoes National Park have received over the years.

"I have been in the hospital twice and I am now unemployed. We sold our house and lost money on it. I do not know if these are just coincidences, but too many things have gone wrong in too short a time. I am not usually superstitious but...please return this lava to its rightful resting place."

—Many thanks, S., Germany

"Enclosed are five lava rocks that my wife and I took from the Big Island during our honeymoon in 1991. We've regretted it ever since. Our luck has been tough the last 13 years, and we've dedicated ourselves to setting things right with Pele. Please return these missing rocks to her along with our apologies." —T. & C.G., U.S.A.

"Since returning from Maui, we have had nothing but bad luck. We are building a house and all of the interior walls have had to be straightened. All of the windows are the wrong sizes. Yesterday one of the workers put a nail through his wrist. This morning my father-in-law fell off of his roof and broke several ribs. Please return these rocks!!"

—M. K., Canada

HELLO KATY

In 2008 Katy Perry rocketed to superstardom with her unique, infectious hit song "I Kissed a Girl," from the platinum album One of the Boys. *Here's Katy's story...and some advice for anyone who wants to follow in this pop star's footsteps.*

STARTING OUT STRICT

On October 25, 1984, Katheryn Elizabeth Hudson entered the world. (She later took her mom's maiden name, Perry, because "Katy Hudson" sounded too much like actress Kate Hudson.) You'd think that such a sassy, outgoing performer would have had a wild youth, but the opposite is true. Katy's parents, who raised her in Santa Barbara, California, were born-again Pentecostal ministers, which meant no MTV, radio, or secular (non-Christian) music were allowed in the house. Katy and her two siblings attended Christian camps, had Christian friends, and sang only Christian songs. Actually, her parents were the ones with the wild pasts: Her mom dated Jimi Hendrix in the '60s, and her dad hung out with counterculture guru Timothy Leary. Perry says that even though she's now following a path that's very different from that of her parents, they're still very close.

THE HARD-WORK YEARS

Anxious to hit the music road, Perry got her GED during

Actress Sarah Michelle Gellar (*Buffy the Vampire Slayer*) has a brown belt in tae kwon do.

her freshman year of high school and devoted her time to taking voice lessons and attending a music academy. Then, at age 15, she flew to Nashville to record a Christian rock album, but it didn't sell well. Two years later, she moved to Los Angeles, where she struggled with more albums that didn't do well…or weren't released at all. In the process, she was signed and later dropped by two major record companies. Still, she kept recording songs (one of which made it onto the soundtrack of *The Sisterhood of the Traveling Pants*) and appearing in other artists' music videos.

CATCHING A ROCKET

In 2007 her perseverance finally paid off when she caught the attention of an executive at Capitol Records. Within a year, her album *One of the Boys* was released, and the single "I Kissed a Girl" spent seven weeks at #1 on the Billboard chart. Suddenly everyone from radio DJs to Madonna was talking about Katy Perry. And she was ready for them: "It's like you catch a rocket and you're hanging on for dear life and you're like, Goooooo!" *One of the Boys* has sold more than seven million copies, and Perry is still going strong: She works 13 hours a day, six days a week, writing and recording songs in addition to performing.

HIGH-ENERGY ADVICE

Katy Perry, now 26, maintains a hectic schedule of touring, recording, TV appearances, and acting (her husband, Russell Brand, is an actor and comedian). What does she do to keep up her spirits—and her energy level—while she's running around like that?

♪ **Treasure hunt.** Known for her anything-goes wardrobe, Perry loves looking for the latest styles, but she's also keen on vintage. One of the advantages of touring, she says, is discovering vintage stores on the outskirts of little towns. "You can buy a dress for $20 and have it tailored for another $20, and still come out ahead." But, Perry warns, if it smells musty, toss it. You can never get that odor out.

♪ **Go organic.** Perry tries to be kind to her body, especially when she's touring from town to town. She avoids fried food and tries to keep her menus healthy and organic with grilled chicken, soy milk…and no chips within viewing range.

♪ **H20.** Water is Perry's real secret to staying healthy. No fruit juices, no sodas—just water. "I drink maybe eight bottles a day."

♪ **Jump.** Perry hates working out but loves to jump rope. Her concerts are about an hour long, so she'll jump rope for a half-hour before each show to get warmed up. It's also a great way to test her revealing outfits to make sure there are no surprise "wardrobe malfunctions."

Scientists estimate that the universe contains more than a trillion galaxies.

♪ **Playing favorites.** When Perry feels stress start to overwhelm her, like when she developed major acne on the 2008 "Warped" tour, she gets a massage or puts on a Madonna song and tries to walk it off. Having her sister, Angela, with her on the road also helps. "She's the person who keeps me in line, whether I like it or not. I trust her and also have a good, healthy fear of her."

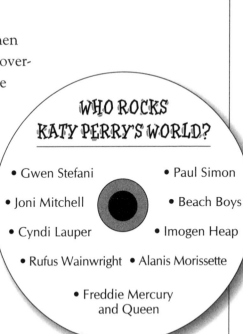

WHO ROCKS KATY PERRY'S WORLD?

- Gwen Stefani
- Paul Simon
- Joni Mitchell
- Beach Boys
- Cyndi Lauper
- Imogen Heap
- Rufus Wainwright
- Alanis Morissette
- Freddie Mercury and Queen

THE DREAM

Recently, when Perry was moving into a new apartment, she found her "vision board," a collage she'd made in the fourth grade that was supposed to represent her dreams for the future. In the center of the board, she had pasted a photo of 23-year-old Tejano music star Selena holding her 1994 Grammy Award statuette. "I knew where I wanted to be even as a young kid," Perry says. "I just didn't know that if I put one foot in front of the other, I would actually get there someday."

GEEKY WEDDINGS

And we thought throwing rice was weird!

ROBO-MINISTER

In June 2007, in Daejeon, South Korea, a cone-shaped robot named "Tiro" became the first machine to officiate at a wedding. (The robot's designer, Seok Gyeong-jae, was the bridegroom.) Tiro, which cost $215,000 to build, has two mechanical arms and a black glass "face" with a mouth of flashing red lights. Tiro introduced the couple to the crowd, then led them through the wedding ceremony. It wasn't the only robot involved in the ceremony—other 'bots acted as ushers, leading guests to their seats.

"I DO!"—TAKE TWO

Nathan and Kelly Davalos, fans of the online fantasy game *EverQuest*, made history when they got married twice in the same ceremony—first in the traditional manner with a human minister, and moments later in the virtual world of *EverQuest*. It all took place at the 2007 SOE (Sony Online Entertainment) Fan Faire in Las Vegas. Flanked by friends costumed as characters from *EverQuest* (with a guest appearance by Darth Vader from *Star Wars*), Nathan kissed his bride in front of 2,000 cheering gamers. Then the pastor invited the newlyweds to "step into their future in *EverQuest*." Logging on to the game, the two said "I do" again in the game's virtual world—and became "Mr. and Mrs. Stormslayer."

FLY ME TO THE MOON

When Erin Finnegan and Noah Fulmor of New York got married in June 2009, the experience had them feeling lighter than air—because they were. The couple exchanged their vows while floating upside down inside the cabin of *G-Force One*, a modified Boeing 727 jet that rose and dipped in multiple arcs to simulate the weightless environment of outer space. The weightless wedding was the brainchild of Zero Gravity Corporation, which offers weightless flights to thrill seekers for $6,000–$8,000 per ticket. Said the happy couple after they'd landed safely, "It was an extraordinary experience, exhilarating, and absolutely the best possible way we can imagine for us to start our new life together."

TORI JOINS THE CIRCUS

Have you ever dreamed of running off and performing under the Big Top? Here's the story of one girl who did just that.

GETTING THE CALL

Tori Letzler wasn't your average 14-year-old. The Westport, Connecticut, teenager had been singing professionally with New York's Metropolitan Opera since she was seven, and she'd already sung the national anthem in front of thousands of people at Philadelphia Phillies and Cincinnati Reds games. So when the call came in 2005 for her to audition for a lead singing role, she wasn't exactly unprepared. But this call was different: It wasn't an opera or theater that wanted her to audition—it was the world-renowned Cirque du Soleil.

NOT YOUR ORDINARY CIRCUS

Cirque du Soleil (French for "Circus of the Sun") is like no other circus in the world. It uses no animals, and the entire show centers around one story line, which is performed on an elaborate and colorful stage. Each show—and there are 23 different productions playing around the globe at any given time—can combine as many as 100 trapeze artists, jugglers, fire-breathers, singers, dancers, acrobats, contortionists, and clowns, all choreographed to dramatic music and lighting. The song lyrics are in many languages (even made-up ones!), so every show can be understood and enjoyed by people anywhere in the world.

SING LIKE A FLEA

The part that Tori tried out for was the role of Zoé in the Cirque Du Soleil show *Quidam*. Zoé is a bored young girl who feels distant and ignored, so she fills her life with a world of imaginary characters. After Cirque du Soleil reviewed a recording of Tori's singing, they invited her in for a grueling live audition. "It was very different," says Tori. "They would say, 'Sing like a flea…a dinosaur…a flea on a dinosaur,' and I knew right away that this was definitely not the Metropolitan Opera." That was just the beginning—the audition process took an entire year before she finally got the part. But it was worth the effort: Tori played the role on tour from 2006 to 2007, performing all over the U.S. and Canada as well as in South Korea, China, and Dubai, in the United Arab Emirates.

CIRCUS LIFE

Life with Cirque du Soleil was nothing like Tori's life at home. Being away from friends and family was tough, but her parents joined up with the circus troupe whenever they could. According to Tori, "Cirque never settles for anything but the best when it comes to housing. Typically we stayed in corporate

…the body releasing growth hormones, usually while you're sleeping.

apartments with all the amenities." And then there was school: Cirque du Soleil provides tutors so that its many young performers and the children of the cast and crew can keep up with their education. Subjects are taught in many languages, and for all grade levels, from kindergarten to high school. Tori's school day would start each morning at 10:00. She and her tutor would work until 1:00 p.m., and after lunch she'd have a few hours to herself to exercise or practice singing. Then at 5:00 p.m., it was time to prepare for that evening's show. Before each performance, Tori had to test sound equipment and work out any changes that had been made to the show. And if the show was opening in a new city, the cast had to practice on the new stage. Then, of course, she had to perform the show—about two hours of singing. And after a performance it usually took her a while to wind down, so she often didn't get to bed until after midnight.

MAKEUP! COSTUMES! ACTION!

In Cirque du Soleil, makeup is just as important as costumes. Many of the performers don't have dialogue, so the makeup helps define the character they're playing. All of the performers, including Tori, were sent to a school in Montreal to learn how to use colored creams, foundations, lipstick, lip liner, mascara, and fake eyelashes, all applied with sponges and brushes. Each artist was taught how to do his or her unique makeup in a step-by-step process. Tori's had 15 steps. "I had the simplest makeup in the show, and the first time I did it myself, it took me two hours." Eventually she was able to get it down to 20 minutes.

THE SHOW MUST GO ON

When Cirque performers are under 18, they're usually asked to share their role with another young person. Tori shared hers with an alternate named Letitia Forbes, a 15-year-old singer from New Zealand. So if Tori ever felt like her voice wasn't up to performing that night, she could rely on Letitia to go on in her place (and then she'd have to stand by in case Letitia got ill or had to stop performing). But Tori, like most performers, didn't like missing her turn onstage. Once, when she got sick during a show, she ran offstage to throw up, then ran back on and kept singing.

Tori left the show in 2006 to finish high school. She went on to attend the prestigious Berklee College of Music in Boston, and in 2009 released her debut CD, *Behind Closed Eyes*. But her time touring with Cirque du Soleil remains one of the best memories of her life. The experience "was an amazing one," Tori recalls. "You get to see the world at such a young age while doing what you love."

For the story of another Cirque du Soleil performer, turn to page 107.

THE SWEET TRUTH

Believe it or not, chocolate is actually good for you.

FOOD OF THE GODS

"Don't eat chocolate—you'll get zits!" "It'll make you fat!" "It's bad for you!" That's what most people think, but—this just in—they're wrong. According to nutrition researcher Michael Levine, "Chemically speaking, chocolate really is the world's perfect food."

But he wasn't the first to realize that: The Aztec and Mayan civilizations were warming up cups of cocoa, or *chocolatl*, more than 3,000 years ago. They believed the cocoa bean improved their health, gave them wisdom, and spiced up their love life. In fact, they called the cocoa bean "food of the gods." When chocolate was introduced to Europe in the late 1500s, Spanish and French aristocrats drank it as a spicy, bittersweet health elixir. Ever since 1938, the U.S. government has made sure soldiers carry chocolate bars, originally called "D Rations." Astronauts take chocolate into space as a prescribed part of their diet. Even Harry Potter, in the best-selling book series, is given chocolate at the Hogwarts infirmary after he encounters Dementors. Why does chocolate pack such a healthy punch? Here are a few reasons.

THE CHOCOLATE FACTS

- Eating chocolate makes the body release a chemical

called serotonin, which calms you and acts as an antidepressant.

• Dark chocolate is jam-packed with the important mineral magnesium.

• Chocolate stimulates production of endorphins, natural chemicals in your body that make you feel happy.

• Chocolate contains theobromine and caffeine, both stimulants that can perk you up.

• Chocolate can improve blood pressure and may reduce the risk of having a stroke or heart attack.

• Chocolate is chock-full of antioxidants—stress-relieving, youth-preserving compounds. So if you're feeling depressed or stressed, a taste of chocolate can help chase the blues away.

WHAT'S NOT GOOD FOR YOU

A milk chocolate candy bar. Milk chocolate is often loaded with lots more than just chocolate, including large quantities of sugar (dark chocolate also has sugar in it), palm oil, and butter. Read the label before you buy: The first two ingredients should always be cocoa and cocoa butter. Sugar can be third. Vanilla's fine. Palm oil and milk products are fattening and can have negative effects on your heart.

NUMEROLOGY 101

Can the secrets of life be found in numbers? Some people think so. With this guide to the ancient practice of numerology, maybe you'll discover a few secrets of your own.

BY THE NUMBERS

Numerology is the belief that our personalities, likes and dislikes, ideal career, and even our future can be determined by the numbers in our lives—specifically, by our birth dates and by numbers that correspond to the letters in our names. Numerology is nothing new; people have been practicing it for centuries, dating back to ancient Greece (and some say it's even older than that). At one time, numerology was considered a legitimate branch of mathematics, but several centuries ago it was dismissed, like astrology, as unscientific wishful thinking. But some people still believe in it. Here's how it works.

DIGIT-AL THINKING

Your *Life Path Number* provides insight into your personality, natural abilities, and hidden talents. In numerology, your Life Path is determined by the numerical conditions present at your birth. To determine your Life Path, all you have to do is reduce your birthday to a single digit, then look up your number on the chart on page 37.

For an example, let's calculate the Life Path Number of First Lady Michelle Obama:

Ms. Obama was born on January 17, 1964.

1. Month: January = 1

2. Day: 17 = 1 + 7 = 8

3. Year: 1964 = 1 + 9 + 6 + 4 = 20 = 2 + 0 = 2

4. 1 + 8 + 2 = 11

5. Reduce 11 to a single digit: 1 + 1 = 2

So Ms. Obama's Life Path number is 2. A quick look at the chart at the end of this article will tell you that she is a natural diplomat and peacemaker.

IT'S DESTINY

According to numerologists, your name on your birth certificate holds a secret code to your destiny—your life ambitions and potential for success. To find your *Destiny Number*, translate the letters of your name into numbers using the following chart. Like you did for your birthday, reduce the numbers to a single digit.

1	**2**	**3**	**4**	**5**	**6**	**7**	**8**	**9**
A	B	C	D	E	F	G	H	I
J	K	L	M	N	O	P	Q	R
S	T	U	V	W	X	Y	Z	

To calculate the First Lady's Destiny Number, we'll use her maiden name, Michelle LaVaughn Robinson:

1. Michelle = 4 + 9 + 3 + 8 + 5 + 3 + 3 +5 = 40 = 4 + 0 = 4
2. LaVaughn = 3 + 1 + 4 + 1 + 3 + 7 + 8 + 5 = 32 = 3 + 2 = 5
3. Robinson = 9 + 6 + 2 + 9 + 5 + 1 + 6 + 5 = 43 = 4 + 3 = 7
4. Add the sums from her name: 4 + 5 + 7 = 16
5. Reduce 16 to a single digit: 1 + 6 = 7

With a Destiny Number of 7, Ms. Obama is someone who appreciates the mysteries of life, and she would make an excellent teacher.

1 2 3 4

NUMEROLOGY CHART

ONE: A natural leader, you have the creativity, courage, determination, and strength to blaze new trails and inspire others to follow you. Use your charisma responsibly.

TWO: As a born diplomat and peacemaker, your empathy inspires solutions to difficult problems. Don't be shy—you might be afraid to step out of your comfort zone to create peace, but you'll be happy you did.

THREE: You are the picture of *joie de vivre*. If life hands you lemons, you turn it into pink lemonade with crushed ice and a cherry on top. Blessed with a gift for words, you're happiest when your creativity inspires others to appreciate the beauty and mystery of life.

FOUR: Stability, dependability, honesty, and super organizational skills are the cornerstones of your

Miley Cyrus's name at birth: Destiny Hope Cyrus.

nature. You also have a knack for money, and will probably have a retirement savings plan before you're 21.

FIVE: Have passport—will travel. Your desire for fun, adventure, and excitement allows you to make friends and money easily. But don't let anyone or anything tie you down—you need your freedom.

SIX: A humanitarian at heart, you are happiest when working for social justice. But remember to take care of yourself, too. Liberate your inner artist and create something beautiful...it's just one of the many hidden talents you have.

SEVEN: Like Threes, Sevens have a profound appreciation for the mysteries of life, but you approach life in a more philosophical, analytical way. You are a student of life and would make a wonderful teacher.

EIGHT: You are networker with a flair for business and an interest in world affairs. Setting goals and meeting them are second nature to you. Remember to have fun on your way up the ladder of success, and make time for your friends and family.

NINE: You may be interested in everything under the sun, but your number-one goal is to make the world a better place. Because your generosity and compassion inspire your actions, you may well find yourself living a life full of service...and beauty.

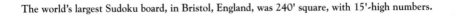

AROUND THE WORLD IN 80 YEARS

Dervla Murphy has traveled to some of the most remote places on Earth armed with little more than her Irish wit, her strong will, and her trusty bicycle.

PEDAL POWER

In 1941, when Dervla Murphy turned 10 years old, she got an Armstrong Cadet bike for her birthday and named it Rocinante, after Don Quixote's faithful horse. (She soon shortened the name to "Roz.") Growing up poor in Lismore, Ireland, Dervla hadn't had much excitement in her life. But as she test-rode her new bike, she had a revelation: "I proudly looked at my legs, slowly pushing the pedals around, and the thought came, 'If I went on doing this for long enough, I could get to India.'" And so the seed was planted for her great adventure.

ON THE ROAD

Murphy had to wait a long time to realize her dream. Her mother, who suffered from severe arthritis, needed constant care. After her mother died in 1962, Murphy, now 31 years old, loaded up Roz and finally hit the road. She wanted her trip to be "self-supporting," as she called it, so she took little more than what she could fit in a backpack—plus a revolver for protection.

She figured that when she ran out of money, she'd take odd jobs until she earned enough to keep going. She wrote later, "The extended hardships and poverty of my youth proved to be a good apprenticeship for this type of travel."

FULL TILT

To get to India, Murphy had to cycle her way across Europe first…and she had no idea that she was riding off into the coldest winter Europe had seen in decades. She

faced harsh weather all through France and central Europe before making her way down the Balkan peninsula to Istanbul. From there she crossed Turkey, Iran, Afghanistan, and Pakistan and, at long last, arrived in India. Along the way, she was chased by hungry wolves in Yugoslavia and forced to fire a warning shot with her gun to fend off a pack of thieves in Iran. But she was constantly impressed by the kindness of strangers: Once, she went to sleep outside in the desert and woke up to find that someone had moved her to a comfy mattress inside an Afghan tent! A talented writer, Murphy collected the stories of her trip in a best-selling book, *Full Tilt: Ireland to India with a Bicycle*, and the money she made enabled her to keep exploring the world. Since then, she has taken dozens of trips, exploring such exotic places as Madagascar and Tibet, and has written more than 20 books about her travels.

FAR FLUNGERY

In 1973 Murphy's five-year-old daughter, Rachel, joined her journeys, beginning with a ride on horseback through the Indus Gorge in Pakistan in the dead of winter. When Rachel grew up, her own two daughters kept up the family tradition by traveling with their grandmother. Now, at more than 80 years of age, Dervla Murphy is still writing books and planning new trips to places she calls "far flungery"—the loneliest spots on Earth, far from phones, televisions, and all the other noisy connecting devices of modern life.

WORDS FOR WANDERERS

Do you dream of seeing the world? You're in good company. Here's what some great thinkers have to say about traveling.

"Security is mostly a superstition. It does not exist in nature…Life is either a daring adventure or nothing."

—**Helen Keller**

"Man cannot discover new oceans unless he has the courage to lose sight of the shore."

—**André Gide**

"I see my path, but I don't know where it leads. Not knowing where I'm going is what inspires me to travel it."

—**Rosalia de Castro**

"Do not follow where the path may lead. Go instead where there is no path and leave a trail."

—**Ralph Waldo Emerson**

"The world is a book and those who do not travel read only one page."

—**St. Augustine**

"I haven't been everywhere, but it's on my list."

—**Susan Sontag**

"One's destination is never a place, but a new way of seeing things."

—**Henry Miller**

"Perhaps travel cannot prevent bigotry, but by demonstrating that all peoples cry, laugh, eat, worry, and die, it can introduce the idea that if we try and understand each other, we may even become friends."

—**Maya Angelou**

In New Guinea, some people use webs of the orb-weaver spider as fishing nets.

FIRST LADIES

Their mission? To go where no woman had dared to go before.

• In 1770 Frenchwoman **Isabel Godin des Odonais** sailed 3,000 miles down the Amazon River from Peru to Brazil, making her the **first woman to cross South America** from the Pacific to the Atlantic. It was no pleasure trip—she was the only member of her 42-person party to survive the fevers, accidents, and tribal attacks that plagued them the entire way. Why did she make such a dangerous trip? She was looking for her husband, a French mapmaker who had been detained by authorities in French Guiana. When everyone else in her group died, Isabel was left alone in the jungle. She wandered for nine days, avoiding jaguars and anacondas, until four native people rescued her. They put her in a canoe and sent her the rest of the way down the Amazon. Amazingly, she found her husband…and they lived together for 10 more years in French Guiana and France.

• In 1871 **Lucy Walker** became the **first woman to scale the legendary Matterhorn** mountain in the Swiss Alps—and she did it wearing only a simple white cotton dress beneath her climbing harness. Born in 1836, Lucy was the first great woman alpinist and logged many ascents in the Alps. Other female climbers wore trousers like the men, but Lucy refused to cramp her style for anyone, or any mountain. As she was making her fourth ascent of the Eiger, another famous Alp, she dined on sponge cake and sparkling wine for the entire expedition. Walker was one of the founders of the Ladies' Alpine Club, and she completed 98 climbs before her death in 1916.

• In 1908 **Annie Smith Peck** became the **first person to reach the 22,205-foot summit of Mt. Huascaran** in Peru, at that time thought to be the highest mountain in South America. That alone was remarkable, but more amazing was that Peck was 58 years old! She took up climbing at the age of 44 and made her last ascent—5,635-foot Mt. Madison, in New Hampshire—at 82. A brilliant academic and lecturer, she fought for women's rights her entire life, and even planted a flag with the motto "Votes for Women!" on top of Peru's Mt. Corupuna (21,079 feet) in 1909.

• In 1936 **Ruth Harkness** became world famous overnight when she emerged from the remote highlands of Tibet with the **first giant panda ever captured alive**. Harkness was the most unlikely of adventurers: She was a New York socialite who, as a friend cracked, "wouldn't even walk a city block if there was a taxi to be hailed." But deep inside, she had a hankering for adventure. After her husband died in Asia while trying to find the reclusive giant panda, she decided to finish his work. So she organized an expedition and hiked 1,500 miles across China and Tibet to find her panda. The rare animal was

Erotographomania is the uncontrollable desire to write love letters.

brought to the Brookfield Zoo in Chicago, where it became the most viewed animal in the zoo's history.

• In 1975 **Junko Tabei** became the **first woman** (and possibly the shortest person—she's only 4'9"!) **to climb Mt. Everest**. She nearly didn't make it out alive—on the way up, at 19,000 feet, she was buried in an avalanche and had to be dug out by her guide. Tabei had weak lungs as a child growing up in Japan and took to mountaineering as a way to build strength and endurance. Climbing became her life's passion. In 1992 she added another first to her name: She became the first woman to scale the Seven Summits, the highest mountains on every continent in the world. Today Tabei, in her 70s, still teaches English literature (when she's not climbing), and has her sights on climbing the tallest mountain in every country in the world…about 196 mountains.

• In 1979 **Dr. Sylvia Earle** set the record for the **deepest solo ocean dive** by a human—1,250 feet. ("Solo" means she was not connected to the surface by any sort of tethering device.) To protect her from the intense water pressure, she wore a specially designed diving suit and air tank. A research submarine took her down to the seabed off the shore of Oahu, Hawaii, and dropped her off. Dr. Earle spent the next 2½ hours wandering the seafloor and gathering biological samples. In reporting her feat, *The New Yorker* magazine gave her the nickname "Her Deepness." But Earle is far more than an adventurer;

Highest-paid TV actresses: the four *Desperate Housewives* ($440,000 each per episode).

she's one of the most prominent marine scientists of the last 50 years. She's led more than 60 expeditions, covering every ocean on Earth and learning so much new information on everything, from whales to ocean algae, that the Library of Congress declared her a "Living Legend." Although navy diver Daniel P. Jackson eclipsed her record in 2005 when he descended to a depth of 2,000 feet, he was lowered from the surface on a cable and did not move around freely, so Sylvia Earle's record for a solo dive still stands.

• In 1988 **Kay Cottee** became the **first woman to sail around the world in an open sailboat solo, nonstop, and unaided.** The 34-year-old Australian grew up around boats, and she always wanted to try her luck at what seafarers consider to be the greatest test of a sailor's endurance and skill. When she left Sydney Harbour in November 1987 at the wheel of her 37-foot boat, *First Lady* (which she mostly built herself), Cottee had only a vague idea of what she was about to endure. At one point during the voyage, a monster wave overturned her boat during a storm, washing her overboard. Fortunately, the two safety ropes she'd used to harness herself to the boat saved her. When she sailed back into Sydney 189 days later, she was greeted as a national hero—she'd traveled farther alone than any other woman in history. Cottee was inducted into the Sailing Hall of Fame, and the *First Lady* is now on display in the National Maritime Museum of Australia.

Popular snack for kids in Siberia: milk popsicles.

HORSE CRAZY

Just a little horsing around.

YOU KNOW YOU'RE A HORSE PERSON WHEN...

- Your horse's mane is perfectly braided, but yours is a mess.
- Mucking out stalls is more appealing than doing homework.
- Your nice clothes are the ones without horsehair all over them.
- You always have a pocketful of carrots and sugar cubes.
- Instead of skipping, you canter.
- You're already drawing horses in the margins of this page.

Newborn foals can't eat grass...their legs are too long for their mouths to reach the ground.

AMAZING!

A couple of racehorses were standing around a stable boasting about their race records. The big bay said, "In the last 15 races, I've won 8 of them!"

The dappled gray tossed his head. "That's nothing. I've won 19 out of my last 27 races!"

"You're lightweights," said the roan, flicking his tail. "Out of the last 36 races, I've won 28!"

Suddenly, a greyhound dog that had been sitting in the corner of the stall cleared his throat. "I don't mean to boast," he said, "but in my last 90 races, I've won 88 of them!"

The horses were stunned. "Omigod!" the gray finally whispered. "A talking dog!"

FA-LA-LA

A sad pony went to the doctor because he couldn't sing. "Don't worry!" said the doctor. "You're just a little hoarse."

HORSE LOGIC

Q. A girl left for a trail ride on Friday, and came back three days later…on Friday. How?

A. Her horse's name was Friday.

The "smiley" emoticon (:-)) was invented in 1982 by a professor named Scott Fahlman.

HORSE FREAK

At 4 feet 10 inches tall and weighing barely 100 pounds, jockey Julie Krone doesn't seem a likely hero in a dangerous sport. But by the time she was voted into the Thoroughbred Racing Hall of Fame in 2000, she'd overcome crippling injuries and years of prejudice. How'd she do it? With skill, hard work...and plenty of horse sense.

RIDE THE HORSEY

Julie Krone clearly remembers the moment when she realized that horses would be the most important thing in her life. Her mother, Judi Krone, an accomplished horsewoman, was trying to sell a palomino in 1965. To convince the buyer that the horse was gentle, she placed two-year-old Julie on the horse's back and let her ride it into the ring. Little Julie did more than that: She reached for the reins and guided the horse around the ring and back to her mother. By the age of five, Krone had already won her first race at a horse show...in the 21-and-under category.

RECKLESS

Julie spent her early years among the horses on her parents' farm in Eau Claire, Michigan. Her family still tells of how she galloped bareback, did flips off her horse, and rode full-tilt into the barn while standing on her horse's back—ducking only at the last minute so she wouldn't hit her head on the door frame. Early on, Krone developed an uncanny understanding of how horses think and feel, which she credits to her relationship with her horse, Filly. "Filly was elusive, naughty, and at times, downright mean," Krone wrote in her autobiography, *Riding for My Life*. "I credit Filly with teaching me to ride well. Just by being her nasty self, she taught me more than any other horse or instructor. There are some things a rider has to learn by touch, by reaction—lessons no instructor can give."

STEP BY STEP

When Julie was 15, she wrote in her diary, "I'm gonna be the greatest jockey in the world because I think I can. I know I can." That summer, she turned down a job with a circus and worked instead as a groom and exercise rider at world-famous Churchill Downs racetrack in Kentucky and at smaller tracks in Ohio, Indiana, and Michigan. A year later, she dropped out of high school and headed for Florida's Tampa Bay Downs to become the professional jockey she knew she could be. The track owners took one look at the tiny blonde and told her she wasn't big enough, let alone old enough, to work at their track. But Julie kept asking, and eventually they gave in. She rode her first winner, Lord Farkle, in 1981, when she was 17. And that was just the beginning.

ROUGH RIDER

Over the next few years, Krone won so many races that at the age of 25 she was already regarded as the best female jockey in history—and made it onto the cover of *Sports Illustrated.* But her ride to the top of the horse-racing world wasn't an easy one. Male jockeys would often crowd her and her horse against the rail during races. Once, when she was about to pass another rider, he grabbed her riding jacket and tugged her backward, then whipped her horse with his crop. Krone let him know how she felt at the postrace weigh-in by shoving him off the scales. When another jockey sliced her ear with his whip, she punched him and broke his nose. "The men just didn't want to be beaten by a little girl," she later wrote. It was truly a school of hard knocks, and she spent a lot of time sorting out which things to let bother her and which ones to just forget.

THRILLS...AND SPILLS

By the early 1990s, Krone had ridden thousands of winners. But one feat had eluded her: She'd never won any of the sport's prestigious Triple Crown races—the Kentucky Derby, the Preakness, and the Belmont Stakes. On June 5, 1993, that dream finally came true when she rode Colonial Affair to victory at Belmont—the first female jockey ever to do it. Two months later, she made history again when she became just the third jockey ever to win five races in a single day at New York's Saratoga racetrack. But she didn't get to bask in the glory for long—

In the Czech Republic, wedding guests throw peas at new brides; in Italy, they throw almonds.

10 days later, she fell in the middle of a harrowing three-horse collision. "If you look at a film of the spill that I took," Krone told ABC Sports, "you can feel the pain that I went through as the horses ran over me. I had fallen in front of them and my body bumped 10 feet in the air as a horse hit me, then I slid across the grass." In that accident, Krone severely bruised her heart and ribs and shattered her ankle. If she hadn't been wearing a protective vest, she probably would have been killed.

REIGNING LADY

After several months of recovery, Krone was back in action and went back to what she did best: winning races. And in 2000 she received the ultimate honor when she was inducted into the Thoroughbred Racing Hall of Fame. Because she's so small, she had to stand on a milk carton to reach the microphone. But the message she delivered was a big one: "I want this to be a lesson to all kids everywhere," she told the crowd. "If the stable gate is closed, climb the fence."

With her victory in the 1993 Belmont Stakes, Julie Krone even impressed horse trainer Scotty Schulhofer, who'd been a longtime opponent of allowing women into horse racing. His comments after her win: "She talks to the horses in body language. They respond to her. I think she's got the finest sense of horses of anyone around."

FOLLOW THAT DREAM

Here are two young women who knew what they wanted… and didn't let anything stand in their way.

GOTTA SURF!

Bethany Hamilton always wanted to surf. Born in 1990, this native of the island of Kauai, Hawaii, won her first championship at age eight and seemed destined for great things. But on October 31, 2003, while 13-year-old Bethany was waiting for a wave, a tiger shark attacked her. The shark bit off a huge chunk of the surfboard…along with Bethany's entire left arm. Her friends helped her get back to shore before she passed out, and by the time they got her to the hospital, the young surfer had lost nearly 60 percent of her blood. But she survived—and 26 days later, she was back on a surfboard. At first, she just wanted to see if she could surf with one arm (she says it's like doing a one-armed push-up), but soon she was competing again. She took second place at the 2003 National Scholastic Surfing Association World Championships, and in 2005 won first place. She turned pro in 2008 and has been a top-20 surfer ever since. Today Bethany travels the world, surfing and inspiring others to go for their dreams. As she says, "Me, quit? Never!"

GOTTA ACT!

Hilary Swank was born in Nebraska in 1974 and lived in

a trailer park outside Bellingham, Washington, until she was 15 years old. By then, the shy but athletic girl (she was an all-state gymnast) had set her sights on becoming an actress. With just $75 in their pockets, she and her mom moved to Los Angeles, where they lived in their car until her mom saved enough money to get an apartment. Hilary soon dropped out of high school to look for acting jobs full-time. To help her get auditions, her mom would take a roll of quarters to a phone booth and make calls to agents. When Swank was 20, she landed a role in *The Next Karate Kid*, but the film got terrible reviews. Two years later, Hilary got a two-year contract to appear on *Beverly Hills, 90210*, and she thought she'd finally made it…but then she was cut from the show. Then, an audition for a low-budget movie called *Boys Don't Cry*—for which she was paid only $75 a day—turned out to be the game-changer. In 1999 Swank won her first Oscar for *Boys Don't Cry*, and her second came five years later for *Million Dollar Baby*, cementing her reputation as a top star. "I don't know what I did in life to deserve this," she said. "I'm just a girl from a trailer park who had a dream."

BRAIN FREEZERS

Try out these rapid-fire riddles on your friends and family. (They'll think you're a genius.)

Q: What has a foot on each side, and one in the middle?

A: A yardstick.

Q: Paul was caught stealing 27 times in one year, but he was never arrested. Why?

A: He was a baseball player.

Q: What travels around the world, but stays in a corner?

A: A stamp.

Q: How many animals did Moses bring on the ark?

A: Moses didn't have an ark; Noah did.

Q: A truck driver went five blocks the wrong way down a one-way street without breaking the law. How?

A: He was walking.

Q: What gets wetter the more it dries?

A: A towel.

Q: What is full of holes, but still holds water?

A: A sponge.

Q: What can run but never walks, has a mouth but never talks, has a head but never weeps, and has a bed but never sleeps?

A: A river.

A newborn baby's strongest sense: smell.

Q: How many months in the calendar year have 28 days?

A: All 12 of them.

Q: Is there a 4th of July in England?

A: Yes, every country has a July 4th.

Q: How far can a dog walk into the woods?

A: Halfway; after that, he's walking out of the woods.

Q: What is a chest without hinges or lid, but inside a golden treasure is hid?

A: An egg.

Q: In which sport do winners move backward and losers move forward?

A: Tug-of-war.

Q: Can a man in California marry his widow's sister?

A: No—if he has a widow, he's dead.

Q: Why are 2010 pennies worth more than 2009 pennies?

A: 2010 pennies has one more penny.

HI FROM SKYE

We interviewed five girls to find out what's hip, what's hot, and what's happening with girls all over the country. Here's our first: Skye, a tall 18-year-old from Oregon who's a Scorpio and loves books. *(For her faves, see page 58.)*

- **Obsession:** Reading
- **Favorite perfume:** Anything with vanilla! Especially Vanille Extreme, a perfume from Comptoir Sud Pacifique that smells like cake. (I like to smell like cake.)
- **Fear:** Cockroaches. Need I say more?
- **Pets:** Two dogs: Glory, a black lab; and Lily, my grandma's Yorkiehuahua.
- **Best gift I ever got:** My friend Liz once put together bags for her friends that she filled with Jane Austen–themed books and jewelry. She even painted romance-novel names on the bags. (Mine was Georgiana.) We all opened them together, drank tea, and watched *Pride and Prejudice*.
- **Coolest thing I've done:** I recently traveled to Ireland and worked on a horse farm for a month. I found the job through a company that matches students with volunteer opportunities.
- **Favorite movie:** *The Princess Bride*.
- **Favorite book:** The Harry Potter series!
- **Celebrity Crush:** James Franco, he is so funny! And pretty good-looking...
- **Quirk:** I have dyed my hair every color in the rainbow, including pink and green.
- **What I'd like to do for a living:** Design costumes, write novels, restore paintings, and possibly be a superhero on the side.
- **Can't live without:** My ukulele! I take it with me everywhere. You never know when you're gonna need to burst into song.

Sharks have no bones, only cartilage.

SKYE'S SIX FAVE BOOKS

We asked our resident bookhound, Skye (see page 57), to talk about her favorite books. She picked some classics… and a few you may not have heard of.

ELLA ENCHANTED by Gail Carson Levine
This retelling of the classic Cinderella story follows Ella of Frell, a girl who was cursed by a fairy at birth to always be obedient. Despite this setback, Ella is a smart and independent heroine who uses her wits to make her way in the world, and takes charge of her own destiny as she sets out to find the fairy who did this to her and have her break the spell. Let's face it, she isn't your average Cinderella, but she still manages to get the prince and leave the ball at midnight…only she does it on her own terms.

THE SISTERHOOD OF THE TRAVELING PANTS by Ann Brashares
The chronicle of one summer in the lives of four best friends as they have their own separate adventures but are kept together by a pair of shared pants. Kind of a

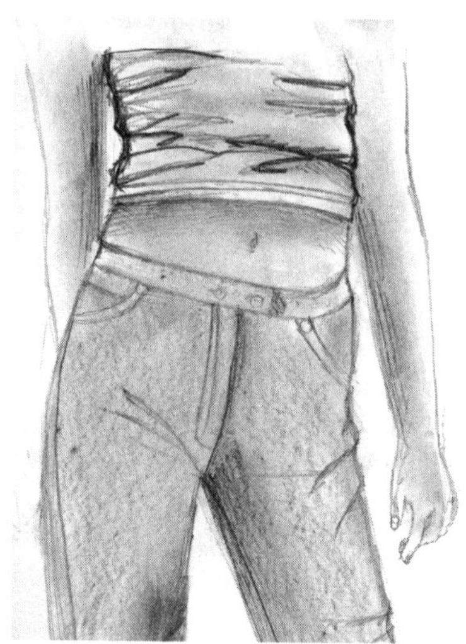

ridiculous concept, I know, but the girls' very different personalities and struggles are what make this book, and leave the reader longing for such a sisterhood. It makes you think about which girl you are most like, and about the sisterhoods you've formed with *your* friends.

ECHO by Francesca Lia Block

A collection of stories that tell about one girl's journey of love and acceptance. Echo has always lived in her beautiful mother's shadow. When she finds a strange, mute boy on the beach, she discovers that she is just as beautiful in his eyes, but she has to live many lives and meet many people before she finds him again. You'll be swept away by this magical book.

I CAPTURE THE CASTLE by Dodie Smith

Unrequited love, two sisters fighting for the same man—one for his love, the other for his money—and a family that may fall apart as the world changes around them. This book sucked me in from the first page. Written in diary form from the younger sister Cassandra's perspective, it tells the story of how her world changes when the owners of the family house, two handsome but very different young men, turn her world upside down. This book will tug on your heartstrings and inspire you to keep a diary of your own.

STARGIRL by Jerry Spinelli

This is the story of how one unique and wonderful girl changes a boy's life and his view of the world forever. Let's face it, school is hard, and most kids just try to fit in. But *Stargirl* does the opposite, and will inspire you to do the same. As you read this, you will want to be Stargirl: play the ukulele, drop pennies on the ground for kids to find, and wear vintage clothes that you customize yourself. It will give you permission to be extraordinary.

THE SECRET GARDEN

by Frances Hodgson Burnett

After the death of her parents, Mary moves to a strange manor in the English countryside. Left to her own devices most of the time, she wanders and finds Colin, a sickly boy, hidden away in the house. Together they unlock the secrets of Colin's past and the door to his dead mother's garden. This is the story of the transformational power of nature and finding a home when you find love.

YOUR OWN SECRET GARDEN

Just about every girl who reads Frances Hodgson Burnett's classic novel The Secret Garden *dreams of having her own private place filled with flowers. Here's how to create one...in your room.*

SUPPLIES

- A shallow container 3 to 6 inches deep (make sure it has a hole in the bottom so excess water can drain out). A pot designed for bonsai (dwarf ornamental plants) will work, but any shallow pot is fine. You can also use a wooden box as long as it has a drainage hole.
- A saucer or plate to put underneath your container to protect your windowsill or table.
- A small bag of fresh potting soil.

WHAT TO PLANT

All kinds of houseplants can thrive in your miniature secret garden. Your local garden center will have lots of small, inexpensive plants perfect for terrariums or dish gardens like yours. Ask for small plants like:

- baby's tears
- Mexican heather
- ferns
- creeping fig
- false aralia
- English ivy
- elfin thyme
- parlor palm

Choose plants of different shapes and sizes. Some of them will be "trees" in your miniature landscape, while others are “shrubs” or “groundcovers.” In general, select plants with very small leaves so they will be in scale with a miniature garden.

HOW TO PLANT

1. Fill the container nearly to the top with fresh potting soil.
2. Moisten the potting soil and position the plants (while still in their plastic pots) until you’re satisfied with how they look together. The plants will grow over time, but set them fairly close together.
3. To remove a plant from its nursery pot, hold the pot upside down and let gravity help you slide the plant out. You can squeeze the bottom of the pot to help get the plant loose, but try not to pull on the plant stem because this can damage it.

4. Use your fingers to punch a hole in the potting soil the same size as the “root ball”—the glob of dirt and roots—of the plant.
5. Insert the root ball into the soil and lightly firm the soil around it with your fingers.
6. After you’ve set in all your plants, water them gently but thoroughly.

MAKE IT MAGICAL

- You can even accessorize your secret garden with small decorative rocks, seashells, or bits of driftwood. Try to imitate nature as you place them.
- For fun, drop in some decorative figurines of animals, fairies, or elves.
- Use scrap wood or popsicle sticks to create fences, benches, or bridges. Craft stores might also carry miniature garden tools or accents such as wheelbarrows or watering cans.
- Fill in bare spots with dried moss, which you'll find at garden centers or craft stores.

"TLC" TIPS

Your garden needs bright light to thrive. Water it only when it needs it, or your plants might end up with "root rot." How do you know when your garden needs water? Push your finger into the soil. If it feels dry several inches down, go ahead and water. It's better to water thoroughly once in a while than to just splash a little water on daily. However, you might want to mist the plants with a spray bottle daily to create "dew" on your enchanted garden. Groom the plants with manicure scissors to keep them small and compact or remove dead leaves. Some of your plants may eventually get too large for your garden. At that point, transplant them into suitable larger pots and refresh your garden with new young plants.

Most users spend an average of 19 minutes a day socializing on Facebook.

THE LANGUAGE OF LOVE

Want to know how to say "I love you" in 19 languages?

Afrikaans	"Ek het jou liefe."
Czech	"Miluji te."
Danish	"Jeg elsker dig."
Ethiopian	"Afgreki'."
Farsi/Persian	"Doostat daram."
French	"Je t'aime."
Gaelic	"Ta gra agam ort."
German	"Ich liebe dich."
Greek	"S'ayapo."
Hawaiian	"Aloha au ia 'oe."
Icelandic	"Eg elska thig."
Italian	"Te amo."
Japanese	"Aishiteru."
Korean	"Sarang heyo."
Mandarin Chinese	"Wo ai ni."
Spanish	"Te quiero."
Swahili	"Naku penda."
Tahitian	"Ua here vau ia oe."
Yiddish	"Ikh hob dikh lib."

EARLY RISERS

Here's a look at three girls who got a very early start…on some very cool careers.

THE FASHIONISTA

Cecilia Cassini lives in Southern California, but this 10-year-old has France in her heart. She's been visiting her grandparents in Paris since she was a baby, and she adores the high fashion the city embodies. "I've always loved Chanel," Cecilia announced on the *Today* show in 2010. Cecilia began modifying her clothes when she was only three (using ponytail holders), and by the age of six, she was begging for her own sewing machine. Her big break came when her mom mentioned the fact that Cecelia made dresses to the owner of a local children's shop. Cecilia soon landed a show there, where she sold 50 handmade pieces. Since then, the young dressmaker has been sewing up a storm, and now has her own fashion line. Her website features pictures of her—wearing her trademark poufy headbands and brightly colored clothes—posing with megastars like Taylor Swift, Miley Cyrus, and fashion designer Diane von Fürstenberg.

THE BROADWAY STAR

Sarah Jessica Parker is most famous for playing Carrie Bradshaw on the TV series *Sex and the City*, but she's been a star since she was in elementary school in Nelsonville, Ohio. At eight years old, "SJ," as her friends call her, landed the title role in the TV movie *The Little Match Girl*. By the time she was 11, she was touring in a national production of *The Sound of Music* with four of her siblings. She made her Broadway debut at age 11, and at 13 played the title role in the Broadway musical *Annie*, singing "The sun will come out tomorrow" night after night for an entire year. After that, her big roles on TV and in numerous hit movies seemed only natural for this veteran performer.

THE CUPCAKE QUEEN

High-school freshman Josie Rea-Tomlinson, whose chocolate cupcake recipe was published in the best-selling cookbook *One Big Table: A Portrait of American Cooking*, believes she was born to be a baker. By the time she was 13, she already had years of baking experience and had even made a wedding cake that fed 150 people. One summer, Josie set out to find the perfect cupcake recipe by baking a new batch nearly every day...and finally found the secret when she realized that she's "not a big fan of numbing by sugar," which happens when you have too much icing. She says, "A simple glaze topping makes a much better cupcake." Just ask Josie's friends at her middle school in California—they love her recipes.

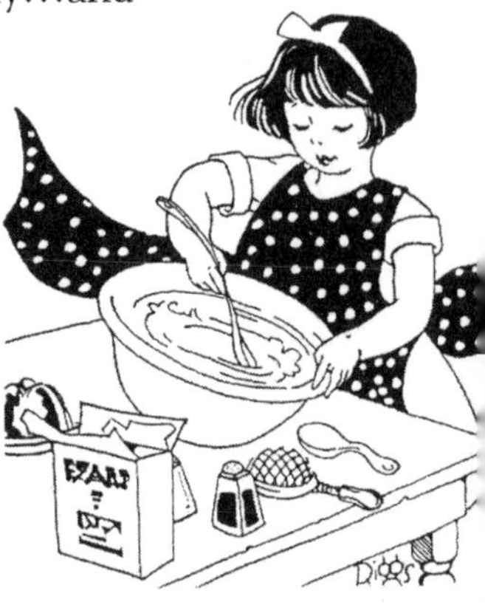

It takes the average 10-year-old about 20 minutes to fall asleep at night.

THE PRINCESS DIARIES, PART I: THE ROYAL PROBLEM

Imagine you're a European princess and you want to get married, and you can only marry someone of royal blood. But all of the royal princes in Europe are your cousins...because your mother, and your mother's mother, and her mother's mother all had the same problem when they were looking for their princes: not enough choices. What happens then? A dirty little royal secret known as "inbreeding."

ALL IN THE FAMILY

There are only a few royal families in the Western world, and they've been marrying each other for thousands (yes, thousands!) of years. In the past, royal marriages were used to cement peace treaties between nations: "My princess of France will marry your prince of England, and then we'll be family and we won't have to go to war with each other." So princesses were often packed off to countries they'd never heard of to marry princes they'd never met. Over time, the ruling houses of Europe married each other so frequently that they became, essentially, one large family.

That resulted in a problem: *inbreeding*—marriage between two people who are close relatives—which comes with a high price. If one person has a physical or mental condition that runs in their family, and they marry a cousin who has the same disease in *their* part of the family, their children are likely to have even bigger problems. And who was the poster family for inbreeding? The Hapsburgs, the Austrian royal family whose influence (and genes) spread throughout Europe from the 1200s to the 1700s.

THE HAPSBURG JAW

The Hapsburgs suffered from *mandibular prognathism*, or the "Hapsburg jaw." This genetic glitch causes the lower jaw to stick out beyond the upper teeth, like a bulldog's. When Hapsburgs married Hapsburgs, their children often developed this grotesque jaw, along with large, misshapen noses, sagging lower eyelids, and stunted bodies. What was worse, many had enormous heads caused by *hydrocephalus*, or "water on the brain," which often causes mental disabilities, convulsions, and early death. But did knowing that these traits ran in the family stop

the Hapsburgs from marrying each other? No—to preserve their power and wealth, they kept on marrying their relatives and passing these genetic traits to royal descendants in Spain, England, Hungary, Bohemia (today's Czech Republic), Greece, Portugal, and even Mexico. Take a look at the portraits of European kings and queens from the 1600s to now, and you'll see the Hapsburgs' pale blue eyes, big nose, and large jaw.

HEMOPHILIA

In the mid-1800s, Queen Victoria of England married her cousin Prince Albert of Germany and had nine children with him. What Queen Victoria didn't know was that she carried a nasty gene that causes *hemophilia*, a serious medical condition that prevents the blood from clotting. This means the smallest cut or bruise can be fatal because it won't stop bleeding. In general, only men get the disease; women with the gene are "carriers," meaning that they don't get sick but pass the disease on to their children. Of Victoria's four sons, only Leopold contracted the disease, and he died at age 30 from bleeding caused by a fall. But two of her five daughters, Alice and Beatrice, were carriers. Unfortunately, Victoria felt that her most important job as queen was to find suitable matches for her children. So Alice and Beatrice dutifully married into the royal houses of Spain and Germany and passed the defective chromosome on to their children and, through them, into the ruling families of Russia, Greece, and Den-

...after 17-year-old female pitcher Jackie Mitchell struck out Babe Ruth and Lou Gehrig.

mark. Today almost every member of the remaining European monarchies is a descendant of Queen Victoria, which means they are all at risk for carrying the deadly gene. One bit of good news: The present royal family of England doesn't have hemophilia—they're descended from Victoria's son Edward VII, who didn't inherit the gene from his mother.

INSANITY

Mental illness was also passed from generation to generation in many royal families. All of the kings of Spain are descended from Queen Juana "the Mad" of Castile (1479–1555), a mentally ill monarch who terrified the people in her court with her screaming rants. Many of her descendants married their cousins or nieces, and that was a recipe for more madness. Another queen, Maria I of Portugal (1734–1816), also earned the nickname "the Mad." She suffered from severe depression and religious mania. The older Maria got, the more unstable she became; in her later years, she dressed up like a little girl and threw temper tantrums in the palace.

BUNDLING

Ever wonder how teenagers dated back in the old days, when people lived way out on farms, with no cars or electricity?

LOVE, EARLY AMERICAN STYLE

If a young man in the 1700s met a girl he liked, he couldn't just take her to the movies. Back then, most people lived in the country, and the girl might live many miles away—miles the boy would have to cover on foot or on horseback to visit her. So a typical "date" might go something like this: Late in the day, he'd walk or ride out to the girl's house, where her family would entertain him with food and conversation. After dinner, when it was too dark for him to make the journey home, he'd stay the night…in the girl's bed.

But it wasn't what you might think. Parents made sure there was no hanky-panky by practicing an old tradition called *bundling*: They'd "bundle" their daughter in a laundry-bag-type outfit that went up to her armpits. Then she'd get under the covers next to the boy, who was also bundled up. Some families even placed a "bundling board" between them—a long plank that allowed for conversation but no funny stuff. Then the young people could talk all night if they wanted to.

As the countryside became more populated, the practice of bundling began to die out; by the early 1900s, it had pretty much disappeared. But the tradition lives on today in some Amish communities.

A single bite from a black mamba snake contains enough venom to kill 200 people.

KiSS ME, YOU FOOL!

It's the last scene of the movie: The girl and the guy finally get together and have a big smooch as the music swells and "The End" rolls up on the screen. But there's more to kissing than just the old smack on the lips. In fact, there are all kinds of kisses.

ESKIMO KISSES

If you want to give someone an Eskimo kiss, you rub noses with them, right? Well...not quite. When Arctic boyfriends and girlfriends greet each other, they press their mouths and noses to the other's cheek and breathe in the scent of that person. That's why in some Arctic languages, the word for "kissing" translates to "smelling." But Native Arctic people aren't the only ones who rub noses: Some Polynesians, Africans, and Asians sniff each other in greeting, too.

A KISS ON THE CHEEK

In most Western cultures, a kiss on the cheek is not a romantic gesture but one of friendship. In Paris it's considered proper to kiss someone on both cheeks at least twice, starting with their left cheek. Over on the west coast of France, in Brittany, the people have a three-kiss pattern, while those on the French Riviera in the south go crazy with five or six kisses! Almost everywhere else in Europe, you start on the kissee's right cheek, kiss once, and then switch to the left cheek, and kiss once more. But the Dutch always end on the right cheek, kissing three times—except when kissing their grand-parents. Then they're supposed to add lots of extra kisses to show how much they love them.

GOTTA HAND IT TO YOU

Ever wonder why men kiss women's hands? It all began in 17th-century Spain, when a gentleman kissed the ring of someone of higher rank as a show of allegiance. This gesture of respect soon spread across Europe: A lady would offer her hand, palm down, to a gentleman, who would bow and lightly touch his lips to her knuckles. Hand-kissing has all but disappeared in western Europe, but it lives on in Romania, Hungary, Poland, and other eastern European countries. And ring-kissing is still with us—when Catholic Church officials meet with the pope, they kiss his ring.

XOXOXO

Signing a letter with Xs and Os means "kisses and hugs"—everyone knows that. But how did that start? In medieval Europe, people who couldn't read or write signed their names with a big bold X—the sign of the cross, meaning that they had taken a solemn oath. To make the oath sacred, the signer would kiss the X. Over the years, the X came to mean a kiss.

Jenny Kissed Me

Jenny kissed me when we met,
Jumping from the chair she sat in;
Time, you thief, who love to get
Sweets into your list, put that in!
Say I'm weary, say I'm sad,
Say that health and wealth have missed me;
Say I'm growing old, but add,
Jenny kissed me.

–Leigh Hunt (1784–1859)

"P" IS FOR PRINCESS

How did author Meg Cabot come to write best-selling novels like The Princess Diaries, Avalon High, *and* Airhead? *In a very roundabout way, actually.*

PUT A PRINCESS IN THERE

Meg Cabot, author of the million-selling *Princess Diaries* series, could easily be crowned the "Queen of Teen Fiction." Her long success list also includes such megahits as *The Mediator*, *1-800-Where-R-You*, *Avalon High*, *Airhead*, and *All-American Girl*. But Cabot didn't always write for teens; her first published books were romance novels for adults. Then a friend, who happened to be a children's book editor, urged her to write a novel for young adults. As Cabot puts it, "I finally wrote about a girl whose mom was dating her teacher, but my friend said that wasn't much of a story. She suggested I write a story about a princess instead. But I was too lazy to write a whole new story, so I just turned the heroine in my story into a princess."

A STRANGER'S ADVICE

Cabot didn't start out as a writer. In fact, she attended Indiana University in Bloomington as an art major. Why? "Because," she says, "a random guy I met at a party in high school told me not to study creative writing because, in his opinion, majoring in creative writing sucks the love of writing out of you. (He was a creative writing major, so he said he would know.) I did not want the love of writing sucked out of me, so I followed his advice. (However, I did take a few creative writing workshops at IU and I enjoyed them very much.) Instead, I had the love of art sucked out of me. Years later, I met that guy from the party again in New York City, where I moved after college to be an illustrator, and we got married."

THE WRITER'S LIFE

Now Cabot, her husband, and their two cats live in Key West, Florida, where she keeps up a feverish pace writing, rewriting, working with publicists, and talking to producers in Hollywood (*The Princess Diaries* has spun off two hit films and *Avalon High* is a TV series). How does she shut out the world and stay focused? Cabot writes in bed in her pajamas, with a can of Tab on the bedside table and earphones on, listening to musicians like Lady Gaga and Vampire Weekend.

COOL FACTS ABOUT MEG CABOT

- She keeps a bag under her bed stuffed full of letters from publishers rejecting her writing. (*The Princess Diaries* was rejected by 17 publishers.)
- She has Lyme disease (not so cool).
- She doesn't have a driver's license.
- She bases all her characters on people she knows (though she tries to disguise them so people won't recognize themselves and get angry).
- On her blog, she refers to her husband as "He Who Shall Remain Nameless."

PRESENTING—THE NUMBER 9

It's the last single-digit number in our counting system...and it's full of kooky surprises.

NATURE

- It takes 9 months to make a human baby.
- A cockroach can live as long as 9 days without its head.
- Water expands by about 9 percent as it freezes.
- The common ladybug has 9 spots.

CULTURE

- Beethoven wrote 9 symphonies.
- There are 9 justices on the U.S. Supreme Court.
- Baseball has 9 players on a team and 9 innings in a game.
- Bart Simpson has 9 spikes of hair.

LANGUAGE AND LITERATURE

- In *The Lord of the Rings* by J.R.R. Tolkien, the race of men is given 9 rings of power.
- There are 9 circles, or levels, of hell in Dante's classic 14th-century poem *The Inferno*.

1. Limbo	**4.** Greed	**7.** Violence
2. Lust	**5.** Anger	**8.** Fraud
3. Gluttony	**6.** Heresy	**9.** Treachery

First U.S. city to add fluoride to its water: Grand Rapids, Michigan, in 1945.

RELIGION AND MYTHOLOGY

- In Christianity, there are 9 types of angels:

Seraphs	Cherubs	Thrones
Dominations	Virtues	Powers
Principalities	Archangels	Ordinary angels

- The ancient Greeks believed there were 9 muses (goddesses of inspiration):

Polyhymnia *sacred poetry*	Thalia *comedy*	Euterpe *lyric poetry*
Calliope *epic poetry*	Clio *history*	Urania *astronomy*
Erato *love poetry*	Melpomene *tragedy*	Terpsichore *dance and song*

THE FORBIDDEN CITY

Because the number 9 is considered lucky in China, Beijing's imperial palace, known as the Forbidden City, has 9,999 rooms. It also has 9 gates, and the boards of each gate are held together in a 9 x 9 nail pattern. The emperors who lived there wore robes decorated with 9 dragons.

GODDESSES RULE: HSI WANG MU

Another "biography" from the days when girl deities ruled.

A PEACH OF A GODDESS

The Taoists of China believe that an earthly paradise lies high in the Kunlun Mountains, in the far west of the country. There, a jade palace is said to perch on a mountaintop, surrounded by a wall of solid gold. This fabulous dwelling belongs to the goddess of eternal life, Hsi Wang Mu. Known as the "Queen Mother of the West," this delicate and beautiful goddess is considered to be the embodiment of *yin*—the feminine.

But Hsi Wang Mu wasn't always such a sweetheart—she came to the Kunlun Mountains as a tiger-woman, spreading pestilence and plague. But after having learning the discipline of the Taoist religion, she was transformed into a gentle, loving goddess. Now she likes to ride a peacock out to her orchard, where she tends a magical peach tree whose branches are so powerful that wizards try to steal them for their wands. The tree bears only one peach at a time, and each one takes 3,000 years to ripen. But the fruit is well worth the wait—a single bite brings the eater 3,000 years of bliss and prosperity. Dozens of Taoist gods and goddesses line up for a bite whenever one is available. After all, a fruit that keeps you going for 3,000 years is everyone's idea of a healthy snack!

Gymnophobia is the fear of being naked.

THE COLOR PURPLE

Purple: It's been called the color of kings. Why? Because for centuries, only those of royal blood were allowed to wear it...and they were the only ones who could afford it.

THE LAND OF PURPLE

Three thousand years ago, fishermen working the shallow waters off the coast of the eastern Mediterranean found a sea snail called a *murex* that had an unusual property: if you squeezed its slug-like body, it oozed a deep, brilliant purple substance that made a beautiful dye. The color became so prized that soon the land where the dye came from—a region we now call Lebanon—became known as Phoenicia, the "Land of Purple." And the dye was named "Tyrian purple" after Tyre, the capital city of Phoenicia. Thanks to that little murex sea snail, the Phoenicians grew very, *very* rich.

PURPLE POWER

It took nearly six million snails to make a single pound of dye, and a single *ounce* of dye cost a pound of gold—in other words, a fortune. As a result, only the very wealthy and powerful could afford purple clothes, and wearing purple became the way for a Phoenician ruler to tell the world he was top dog. Soon purple also became the royal color of the empires of Egypt, Persia, and Rome. And when the Catholic Church replaced the

Ovaltine's original brand name: Ovomaltine.

Roman Empire as the most powerful institution in Europe, the popes adopted purple for their holy robes.

SAVE THE SNAILS

By the 5th century A.D., purple clothes were in such demand that the murex snail population was on the verge of being wiped out. Emperors, kings, and popes started looking for alternatives to Tyrian purple—and they found one. In 1464 the Catholic Church introduced what became known as "cardinal's purple," a maroon dye made from a small insect called a *kermes* (which also gave its name to the new dye's color, *carmine*). A hundred years later, the Spanish brought another insect-derived dye—*cochineal*—back from their conquests in Mexico and Peru. Once again, fabrics made from these luxury dyes were available only to the rich and the royal.

MAUVE OVER, DARLING

But in 1856, an accidental discovery brought purple to the people. That year, an 18-year-old chemist named Sir William Henry Perkin was trying to create a new medicine for malaria when he mixed together several chemicals and found not a cure...but an unusually beautiful purple dye. His family saw the commercial potential for Perkin's discovery, which they named *mauvine*, or *mauve*, and within a year they opened their first dye factory.

Soon, "Mauve madness" took over in the ballrooms of Europe, especially after Napoleon III's wife, Empress Eugénie, was seen wearing it. Then England's Queen Vic-

Janet Guthrie, the first woman to race in the Indy 500 (1977), was once an aerospace engineer.

toria got into the act when she appeared at her daughter's wedding in 1858 in a mauve gown. This new dye was inexpensive and easy to make, and soon ordinary people from all walks of life were going purple, just like royalty.

PURPLE POINTS OF FACT

- When Cleopatra went to visit the Roman general (and, later, her boyfriend) Mark Antony in 41 B.C., she arrived on a boat with silver oars and purple sails. (More than 10 million snails gave their lives for those sails!)
- Every Roman emperor wore a purple toga trimmed with gold embroidery. But even emperors had to watch their budgets: In the 3rd century A.D., when Emperor Aurelian's wife wanted a purple silk toga of her own, he flat-out refused, saying, "That will cost its weight in gold!"

* * *

COUGH-Y BREAK

One night in 2001, 97-year-old Gladys Adamson of Cambridge, England, was struck with a coughing fit so severe that it lasted several hours. The next morning, she went into the bathroom and looked at herself in the mirror. The strange thing about that was—Adamson had been blind for five years. Doctors figured the coughing had something to do with restoring her sight, but exactly how it happened is still a mystery.

WILL YOU MARRY ME?

There's more than one way to ask someone to marry you. Here are a few from around the world.

STEP INTO MY BLANKET

According to Sioux tradition, a young man would court a girl he fancied by playing his flute outside the girl's tepee. If she ignored him, that meant "No, thanks." But if she stepped outside her tepee to listen, that was a good sign. And if she opened the blanket she wore around her shoulders and invited him to embrace her, that was a *very* good sign—it meant that they were engaged, and a wedding was just around the corner.

WANT TO WRESTLE?

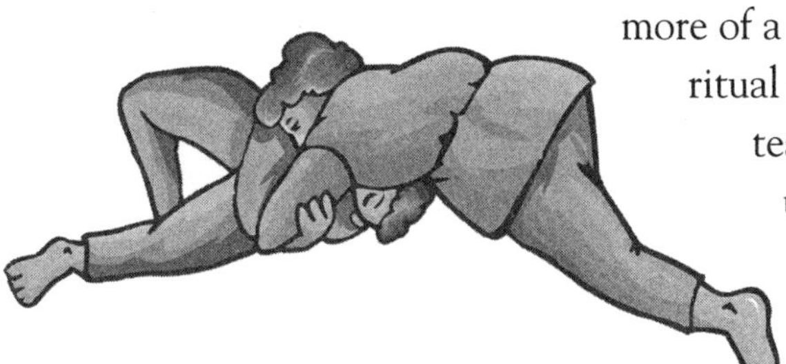

Girls in the ancient Greek city-state of Sparta had it good. They learned to read and write, were allowed to own land, and learned wrestling and gymnastics. The only downside: Before she got married, a Spartan woman was expected to wrestle her prospective husband in public as a test to see whether she was strong enough to be married to him. It was more of a wedding ritual than a contest, and it usually ended with the man carrying off his future bride. But it showed that strength and fitness were valued in a wife and mother.

IF YOU WANT IT, PUT A KNIFE IN IT

A thousand years ago, Norse fathers had an interesting way of letting the world know their daughters were available for marriage: They had the girl wear an empty knife sheath on her belt. If a Norse guy was interested, he'd put his knife in the sheath and—just like that—they were engaged.

GLOVES ON

When an English man in the 18th century wanted to propose to his sweetheart, he'd send her a pair of his gloves. If she showed up at church the following Sunday wearing them, it meant the answer was yes.

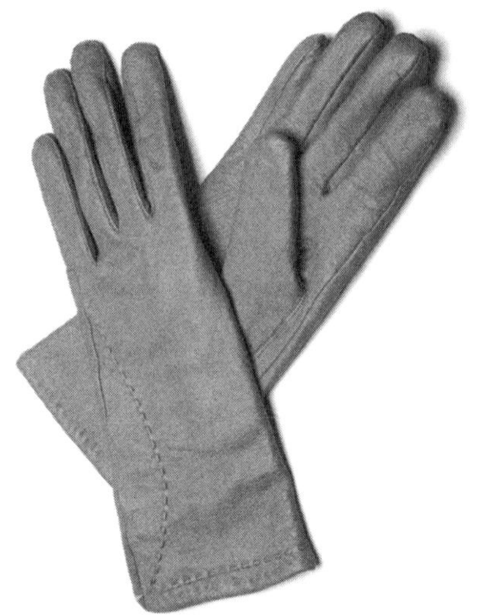

> "I've been looking for a girl like you—
> not you, but a girl like you."
> —Groucho Marx

UKE GIRL

What do you get when you combine a talented girl, a big voice, a ukulele, and a YouTube account? Internet phenom Julia Nunes, that's who!

THAT'S SEVEN A'S!

New Yorker Julia Nunes (pronounced "Noons") comes from a musical family. Her piano-playing dad writes children's songs, and both of her grandfathers were musicians. Julia learned to play the piano when she was seven, and later picked up the guitar. In 2005, when she was 16, Julia took up the ukulele because it was easy to dance with—and she loves to dance. A year later, she filmed a few videos at home and in her dorm room at Skidmore College of herself playing ukulele and singing songs written by other artists, as well as some of her own original tunes. On March 21, 2006, she started posting them on YouTube under the user name "jaaaaaaa," which she says was the result of accidentally holding down the "a" key after typing her first initial.

TO THE INTERNET...AND BEYOND

It wasn't long before YouTube fans were buzzing about Julia's cool videos. Soon others took notice, including the head honchos at Bushman, an Indiana company that makes ukuleles. They encouraged Julia to enter their World Ukulele Video contest in 2008, which she did—singing "Survivor" by Destiny's Child. Not only

The *Harriet the Spy* books have been banned in several U.S. cities for "teaching kids to spy."

did she win the contest (and a free ukulele), but her YouTube fan base snowballed.

SUNSHINE GIRL

One morning Julia learned that a song she wrote, "Into the Sunshine," had received more than a million hits. "I had just woken up and was like, 'Whoa, this is weird,'" she recalled. "'I don't get why people are watching this, but OK.'" One of the million hits was from alternative-rock star Ben Folds (one of Julia's idols), whose manager gave her a call. Folds liked her cover of his song "Gone" and wanted her to open for him on tour in spring 2008. "They were like, 'Is it Noo-nez or Noons? We want the team to say it correctly.' I was like, 'There's a team?!'"

TOP OF THE POPS

Five years after posting that first YouTube video, Julia has three albums and several tours under her belt, and 23,000 subscribers to her YouTube site. Her videos have been viewed more than 43 million times. Thousands line up for her sold-out concerts in London, New York, Nashville, and other cities around the world...and rock stars do covers of *her* songs. What does the future hold? In a recent interview, Julia said, "I've always just been reluctant to let go of Plan A, which was to graduate college, get a desk job, and pay my parents back for my tuition. But I wouldn't mind making music Plan A, and I think I'm going to give it a try."

GROANERS

These jokes are so bad…that they're perfect for annoying your friends.

Q: Why does Peter Pan always fly?

A: Because he can Neverland.

Q: What did baby corn say to mommy corn?

A: Where's popcorn?

Q: What did the left eye say to the right eye?

A: Between you and me, something smells.

Q: How many ears does Davy Crockett have?

A: Three: a left ear, a right ear, and a wild frontier.

Q: What kind of animal goes OOM?

A: A cow walking backward.

Q: The customer asked, "Do you serve crabs here?"

A: "Yessir," replied the waiter. "We'll serve just about anybody."

World's first MySpace account: a user named "ducky," who now has over 200,000 friends.

GIRL INVENTORS

Say "inventor," and the first name you think of might be Thomas Edison. But some of the world's coolest new inventions come from the minds of girls.

INVENTOR: Rachel Zimmerman
INVENTION: A printer that helps kids with speech disorders communicate
STORY: In the mid-1980s, 12-year-old Rachel was looking through books about Helen Keller and Louis Braille when she learned about another pioneer in communication, Charles Bliss. Shortly after World War II, Bliss invented a language made up of pictures and symbols that could be understood by people who didn't speak the same language. "Blissymbolics" was soon adopted by schools to help teach kids with cerebral palsy and other disorders how to communicate with each other. Rachel, a sixth-grader from London, Ontario, Canada, got curious about Blissymbolics and taught herself how to draw the symbols on a computer. The following year, she invented the Blissymbol Printer, a device that allows the user to "write" a sentence as a sequence of pictures on a special touch pad, and then print it out in English. Rachel's Blissymbol Printer not only won her seventh-grade science fair—it also won a silver medal at Canada's World Exhibition of Achievement of Young Inventors in 1985. Her invention was a huge leap forward for Blissymbolics and

has helped countless kids with disabilities communicate via computers and through e-mail.

INVENTORS: Asil Abu Lil, Nour Al-Arda, and Asil Shaar
INVENTION: An obstacle-detecting cane for blind people
STORY: The streets of Nablus, in the West Bank of the Palestinian territories, are narrow, steep, and full of potholes. After watching her blind aunt and uncle struggle to get around with simple walking sticks, a 14-year-old Palestinian girl named Asil Abu Lil decided there had to be a better way. With the help of classmates Nour Al-Arda and Asil Shaar, she devised a solution: a cane with two infrared sensors that beeps whenever it detects an obstacle or hole. To get the parts they needed, the girls had to make several trips to the town of Ramallah, 45 minutes and two Israeli military checkpoints away. But it was worth it: In April 2000, their special cane won the girls a trip to a youth science fair in the United States and a chance at a $75,000 grand prize. One problem—there was only enough money for two of the girls to make the journey to San Jose, California. The three of them drew straws, and Asil lost—she would have to stay home. But luckily, workers for the United Nations found out about the girls' dilemma and raised the money to buy a third ticket. When asked why it was so important for all three of them to go, U.N. spokesman Chris Gunness said, "These girls are the Albert Einsteins of tomorrow."

The Japanese have devised a smiley face that can be read without turning sideways: {*_*}

INVENTOR: Krysta Morlan

INVENTION: A "cast cooler"

STORY: "Growing up with cerebral palsy made me a stronger person and very determined to succeed," says inventor Krysta Morlan. Krysta was 15 years old when she came up with her first invention: the Cast Cooler. Because of her condition, Krysta has endured nearly a dozen surgeries and often has to wear uncomfortable hip and ankle casts during recovery. With her dad's help, Krysta modified an aquarium pump, a small battery-powered motor, and a slim plastic tube to force air into the cast and help cool the patient's skin, which can get

hot and sweaty cooped up inside a cast for weeks on end. She was awarded the prestigious Lemelson-MIT Invention Apprenticeship and used the prize money to create her next device: a semisubmerged "water bicycle" for use in physical therapy. Thousands of people with disabilities now have Krysta to thank for helping to make their recovery time and therapy less uncomfortable and more fun.

INVENTOR: Abbey Fleck

INVENTION: A microwave bacon rack

STORY: On a Saturday morning in 1993, Abbey Fleck of St. Paul, Minnesota, was cooking bacon with her dad. When he ran out of paper towels to soak up the grease, he grabbed the morning newspaper to finish the job. According to Abbey, her mom freaked out that he was going to let newspaper touch their food, which prompted her dad to quip, "I could just stand here and let it drip dry." That gave Abbey an idea: What if you could cook the bacon while it was hanging, and then capture the grease in a bowl? And that's how the Makin' Bacon was born. The device features three T-shaped "drip bars" over a microwave-safe bowl that catches the excess grease. Makin' Bacon became an instant hit and was featured in *Parade Magazine*, *Good Housekeeping*, and even on TV shows like *Dateline NBC*, *The Today Show*, *David Letterman*, and *Oprah.* Not bad for an eight-year-old.

THE COW WHISPERER

She's a professor of animal science, a best-selling author...and the most famous autistic person on the planet. Meet Temple Grandin.

BEING DIFFERENT

As an autistic child growing up in the 1950s, Temple Grandin lived in a world of her own. Like many kids with autism, a psychological condition that makes it difficult for them to communicate and interact with others, she couldn't speak until she was five and had trouble responding to other people. She also panicked at noises and couldn't bear to have anything touch her skin. Her future seemed hopeless. But when Temple was 16, her mother sent her to spend the summer on her aunt's farm—and the experience changed her life.

CATTLE CALL

One day Temple was watching her aunt's cows getting vaccinated. They were nervous and jumpy, and to keep them calm, farmworkers ushered them, one by one, into a "squeeze chute," a cage that hugs a cow while it's given a vaccine shot. Temple saw that many of the cows relaxed almost instantly, so she decided to try it herself. Normally, the lightest touch was agony for Temple, but the squeeze chute provided a deep-pressure touch that actually calmed her down. She stayed in the chute for half an hour and felt calm for more than an hour afterward. The benefits were so great that later on, Temple built her own box, outfitted with padded foam-rubber sides, which she called the Big Squeeze. She still uses it about once a week. As she puts it, "The Big Squeeze helps me have nicer thoughts."

ANIMAL INSTINCTS

Grandin's emotions work differently from most people's, and she feels constantly anxious. When she was working with her aunt's cattle, she realized that she experiences life a lot like animals do. Fear is the main emotion of animals in the wild because it motivates them to flee from predators. And things that scare animals—sudden movements, fleeting shadows, a coat flapping, or a plastic bag blowing in the wind—also scare people with autism. Horses rear up, cows bellow...and people with autism panic.

Scientists have theorized that animals process the world around them in a way that's similar to how Grandin and other people with autism do—in visual images, rather than in language-based thoughts. So if a horse has a bad experience in a barn with a skylight, he may fear all barns with skylights, but will be fine in a barn with a solid roof. It's Grandin's understanding of how animals, particularly cows, perceive the world that led her to invent something in the 1990s that changed the world—a design for humane livestock-handling facilities at meat-processing plants.

COW'S-EYE VIEW

To build better livestock chutes, Grandin needed to understand why cows were so afraid of fencing, as she'd observed on her aunt's farm. So she went to a cattle-processing plant, got down into the chutes with a camera, and took pictures to get a cow's-eye view. Then, she says, "I began to see the sort of things that would bother the cattle: a shadow, a little thread out of place, any little thing, a coat or a hat hanging on the fence, that would make them balk." Loud noises and bad lighting, she found, would cause them to spook even more.

So she designed a *curved* chute system, where the cows walk through rounded pathways and can't see people up ahead; they just keep following the animal in front of them. There's no fear, no bellowing; it's practically silent. Now, more than half of the cattle that go to market in North America are handled in systems that Grandin designed.

BEING DIFFERENT MAKES A DIFFERENCE

Today, Temple Grandin is a professor at Colorado State University and is recognized as one of the world's leading experts in animal behavior. She's also a best-selling author and travels the world giving lectures and teaching. Grandin says that she'd never want to be "cured" of her so-called disorder. "If I could snap my fingers and become nonautistic, I wouldn't do so," she says. "Autism is part of who I am."

COOL SCHOOLS

In one summer, you could become a firefighter, an elfologist, and a space cadet. All you have to do is visit these unusual schools.

CAMP FULLY INVOLVED

School: New Hampshire Fire Academy

Location: Concord, New Hampshire

If you're between the ages of 14 and 20 and think breaking down doors, charging into burning buildings, and putting out fires sounds like fun, then look no further: Camp Fully Involved is the summer vacation for you. This hands-on, physically challenging program is just what you'd expect firefighting to be. During the week, you get to rappel down buildings, climb 100-foot ladders, knock ventilation holes into ceilings, fight fires, and wear all the cool gear firefighters wear. No experience required—just a passion for saving lives. Oh, one more thing: Camp Fully Involved is for girls only.

ÁLFASKÓLINN

School: Icelandic Elf School

Location: Reykjavik, Iceland

The nation of Iceland is known as the "land of fire and ice" because of the snow-covered volcanoes that dot its landscape. According to local legend, it's also home to invisible, mythical men and women known as the *huldufólk*, or "hidden people." The *huldufólk* are thought to look and sound like humans, but they dress in old-fashioned clothes and live in rocks and crags. If you want to learn more about them, you can take a daylong class at the Álfaskólinn. Headmaster Magnus Skarphedinsson will spend an afternoon telling you tales about *huldufólk*, elves, gnomes, and other creatures from Icelandic folklore. You'll get your very own textbook and a tour of some local "elf sites." Best of all, you get a diploma in "elfology." It's a fun day, and it gives you a peek into the culture of the Icelandic people.

SPACE CAMP

School: U.S. Rocket and Space Center

Location: Huntsville, Alabama

Do you dream of being an astronaut? At Space Camp, you can spend a week learning how to pilot a space shuttle, land a lunar module, repair a broken solar panel on the Hubble Space Telescope, take a space walk, and be the first human to step on the planet Mars—all using the same simulators that real astronauts train with for their missions. Space Camp is run by the U.S. Rocket and Space Center Museum's education program as a way of encouraging young people to learn more about math and science. Programs are varied to accommodate kids of all ages, and even adults. More than half a million people have attended Space Camp since it opened in 1982.

A bottlenose dolphin's brain is bigger than a human's.

LOVE, VICTORIAN STYLE

In England's Victorian era (1837–1901), if a young gentleman wished to meet a certain young lady, he couldn't just stroll up to her and say hello. He had to "court" her—a formal process with very strict rules. Here's how a typical courtship went in the 1800s.

Step 1: Be formally introduced

At a social event like a ball or party, the young man sees an interesting lady from across the room. Now he has to find someone of good character—someone who knows her already—to introduce him to her.

Step 2: Make the first move

If the introduction goes well and the man wants to get to know her better, he gives her his calling card (a small card with his name printed on it) and lets her know he'd like to escort her home after the party.

Step 3: Follow it up

At the end of the evening, the young lady, who may have received numerous cards from interested gentlemen, reviews her options. Then she presents her own card to the young man she wants to escort her home, and he rides in the carriage with her and her chaperone, his own carriage following.

Step 4: Get to know each other better

If the young lady and gentleman hit it off, then the

gentleman makes several visits to her home in the following weeks. Their visits are *always* chaperoned by one of the girl's relatives, usually her mother or an aunt.

Step 5: Get serious

After many visits, if the courtship becomes more serious, the couple might be permitted to sit and talk on the front porch alone (with the girl's parents watching through a window). Eventually, they might even get to take a few unsupervised walks.

Step 6: Take the plunge

If the young man decides he wants to ask for the young lady's hand in marriage, his proposal has to be made in writing and presented to her father first.

Step 7: Dot the i's, cross the t's

If Dad and daughter accept, the number-crunching begins. Representatives of both families examine the income and wealth of the other to make sure the marriage will be financially beneficial to both sides. Ancestries are inspected to confirm that both come from "good" families. If everything checks out, the couple quietly becomes engaged, and the young man presents the lady with a ring. She sometimes gives him a ring in return.

Step 8: Time to party

Engagement parties are held so that the prospective groom can meet the bride's relatives, and vice versa. These events formally announce the engagement to family, friends, and the public.

Step 9: Count down the days...or years

An engagement can last from six months to two years, during which time the couple may walk, talk, and ride in a carriage alone. He may put his arm around her waist; she can rest her head on his shoulder. They can hold hands and even exchange a brief kiss or two.

Step 10: Live happily ever after

At last the couple weds and, after a brief honeymoon, moves into their new home. They send wedding cards to family and friends, letting them know that they can now visit the newlyweds. During each visit, wedding cake is served and toasts are made to the couple's happy future.

...that he was color-blind.

"H" IS FOR *HUNGER GAMES*

Picture a futuristic society in which the United States has been destroyed, many people live in crushing poverty, and boys and girls fight to the death on live TV. Who turns a strange idea like that into a best-selling novel series? Suzanne Collins, that's who.

REALITY TV

According to author Suzanne Collins, the inspiration for her smash-hit book *The Hunger Games* came one evening when she was channel surfing. Switching between reality TV and actual war coverage, she noticed that on one channel, kids were competing for money, while on the other, young people were fighting for their lives. Collins was tired, and the lines between the programs began to blur in an unsettling way. She began imagining a young girl in a dark civilization filled with poverty, starvation, and the aftereffects of war.

ROOTED IN THE PAST

Soon Collins found that a Greek myth started creeping into her story. In the myth, the city of Athens periodically sends seven boys and seven girls to Crete, where they are thrown into a labyrinth inhabited by the ferocious Minotaur (half man, half bull) and instructed to find their way out...or be eaten by the monster. The young people never manage to escape the labyrinth

In Japan, many restaurants serve women smaller portions than men, for the same price.

until, one day, a boy named Theseus volunteers to go in their place…and he defeats the Minotaur and finds his way out. Collins says that, in her own way, her heroine Katniss Everdeen is a futuristic Theseus, and the Hunger Games themselves are an updated version of the Roman gladiator games. In fact, Collins chose her future world's name, Panem, from the Latin phrase *panem et circenses*—"bread and circuses"—an ancient Roman catchphrase for one way that a devious politician could rise to power: by offering food and violent entertainment to the poor.

PUTTING IT TOGETHER

When Collins became famous with *The Hunger Games* and her other best-selling series, the *Underland Chronicles*, she had already been a professional writer for some time. She began her career in children's television, where she wrote for such popular shows as *Clarissa Explains It All*, *The Mystery Files of Shelby Woo*, and *Clifford's Puppy Days*. Then one day, a colleague suggested she give children's books a try. Collins got to thinking about *Alice in Wonderland* and what it would be like if it were set underneath a city—and she came up with *Gregor the Overlander*, the first of five books in her *Underland Chronicles* series. A few years later, she came out with *The Hunger Games* and two sequels, *Catching Fire* and *Mockingjay*—and the rest is million-selling history.

JUST DO IT

How does Collins write such wildly popular novels?

Well, workdays at her house in Connecticut begin a lot like they do everywhere else: with a bowl of cereal. But then she makes a beeline for the computer and starts writing. Some days she writes for three to five hours, and some days she just stares at the wall (though she says that's good too, because her brain is still working hard). And while some authors just make up their stories as they go, Collins says, "I've learned it helps me to work out the key structural points before I begin a story. The crisis, climax, those sorts of things. I'll know a lot of what fills the spaces between them as well, but I leave some uncharted room for the characters to develop. And if a door opens along the way, and I'm intrigued by where it leads, I'll definitely go through it."

What does the future hold for Suzanne Collins? For starters, the *Hunger Games* movies—three of them—are expected to debut in 2012.

WHAT DID SUZANNE COLLINS READ AS A KID?

A Wrinkle in Time, by Madeleine L'Engle

Dandelion Wine, by Ray Bradbury

A Tree Grows in Brooklyn, by Betty Smith

The Heart Is a Lonely Hunter, by Carson McCullers

1984, by George Orwell

Anna Karenina, by Leo Tolstoy

Slaughterhouse-Five, by Kurt Vonnegut

Lord of the Flies, by William Golding

Boris, by Jaap ter Haar

Germinal, by Emile Zola

According to Mattel, Barbie attended Willows High School in Willows, Wisconsin.

I'M LILY FROM "MINNE-SNOW-TA"

Next up in our "real girl" interviews: Lily, a 16-year-old who lives in Minnesota (or, as she calls it, "Minne-snòw-ta"). Her claim to fame: She once "mushed" a dogsled pulled by 20 very energetic racing dogs! Here's more about Lily, in her own words…

- **Beginnings:** I'm half Native American. My Ojibwa birth name is Nabagoshk Wanakeewin, which means "Lily, Bringer of Peace." I was named by an elder of my tribe when I was eight months old. Good thing my parents had already named me Lily!
- **Obsession:** Dogs, definitely. I have a Brittany named Dragon that I've raised from birth. He's tan and white, and super smart.
- **Other pets:** April, our sweet old black spaniel, and two cats: Sugar, a mix we adopted from the Humane Society, and KiKi, a Persian who adopted us.
- **In my spare time:** I love to draw, especially (what else?) dogs. (You can see two of my sketches on these pages.)
- **Fave food:** Pizza with mushrooms. I also love to bake chocolate-chip cookies.
- **Favorite activity:** Shopping. (Isn't it everybody's?)
- **Fave old movie:** *Bubble Boy*, with Jake Gyllenhaal.
- **Fave books:** I love the *Golden Compass* series. They're fun to read and reread.
- **Sports:** I've played soccer since I was four.

- **Summer job:** Junior camp counselor at a nature center in Minneapolis. I love working with little kids.
- **For fun:** I trained Dragon to pull me on my bike. He'd make a great sled dog!
- **Inspiration:** Cesar Millan, the Dog Whisperer. He's the best!
- **Biggest fear:** Heights. I hate flying.
- **Pet peeve:** Rain. Give me a good Minnesota snowstorm any day.
- **What I want to do:** Work with animals, be a dog trainer. (Big surprise!)

Lily's 10 Fun Facts about Dogs

1. Tallest breed: Irish Wolfhound.
2. Smallest breed: Chihuahua.
3. Fastest dog: Greyhound.
4. Smartest dog: Border Collies are recognized as the smartest breed. A female named Chaser from South Carolina knows more than 1,000 words!
5. Oldest living dog: Pusuke, a cross-breed who lives in Japan, is 25!
6. World's ugliest dog: Chinese Crested Dog. This breed has the most wins at the annual World's Ugliest Dog Contest in Petaluma, California.
7. Chow Chows have blue-and-black tongues.
8. Dalmations are born white, then develop black spots.
9. Basenjis don't bark; they yodel.
10. What country has the biggest dog population? The United States.

EXTREME ATHLETES

Meet four gutsy women who risk it all for the thrill of some very *dangerous sports.*

JEN "WHO DAT?" HUDAK

Sport: Freestyle skiing

Jen's Story: Jen, who was born in 1986 and started skiing just three years later, describes herself as "an environmentally friendly, nerdy, loud, people-loving jock." This five-time X-Games medalist is a perfectionist—she'll spend hours on the computer studying videos of a single trick, just so she can do it better next time. If you think skiing halfpipes and superpipes is all fun, consider this: At last count, Hudak has been to the hospital more than 23 times because of various falls, and has had five surgeries: four on her knees, and one on her elbow.

STEPH DAVIS

Sport: Rock climbing

Steph's Story: Most rock climbers do their climbing with a partner so there's someone to catch them if they fall. But Steph Davis believes "fear is the danger"—and began climbing by herself, with only a rope. She became the first woman to make a solo climb of Yosemite's Salathé Wall on the famous El Capitan rock formation, and then she went one step further: She got hooked on "free soloing"—climbing steep cliffs without using any ropes at all. Davis's specialty is scaling cliffs as high as

In 1933 Pope Pius XI condemned women who attended boxing matches for being unfeminine.

400 feet—and then leaping off the cliff and floating to the ground with a parachute.

DANICA "LUCKY #7" PATRICK

Sport: Auto racing

Danica's Story: When she was 10 years old, Danica Patrick started racing go-karts in her native Wisconsin. Sixteen years later, when she crossed the finish line at the 2008 Indy Japan 300, she became the first woman to win an IndyCar race. (IndyCars are the long, aerodynamic autos that are used in the Indianapolis 500.) And, to put the icing on the cake, Patrick raced in the 2009 Indianapolis 500—and took third place, the best finish by a woman in the race's history.

JESSICA WATSON

Sport: Sailing

Jessica's Story: On May 15, 2010, this 16-year old Australian steered her 34-foot sailboat, *Ella's Pink Lady*, into Sydney Harbour, ending a sailing trip that lasted 210 days and 20,000 miles—making her the youngest person ever to sail solo around the world, nonstop, without assistance. The journey was filled with intense loneliness, bad weather, and 40-foot-tall waves that threatened to overturn the boat, but Jessica sailed on. Critics had argued that she was too young to attempt the trip, but she proved them wrong. Says Jessica, "I hated being judged by my appearance and other people's expectations of what a 'little girl' was capable of."

SKATER GIRL

What does a world-champion in-line skater do with her talents besides compete? In Katie Ketchum's case, she joins the circus.

GOING TO X-TREMES

Buffalo, New York, native Katie Ketchum started in-line skating in 1999, when she was 15. Within a year, she was competing in in-line park events—competitions where skaters string together aerial maneuvers and tricks using the banks, drops, and edges of the park. Early in her career, Katie became the first girl to land a 900 (2½-rotation turn) in the Aggressive In-line Skating category. After dominating the women's divisions, she began competing against male skaters (the men's divisions have bigger cash prizes). In 2005 she finished seventh in the Men's In-line Park event at the Asian X-Games, an extreme-sports competition sponsored by ESPN. And it wasn't a fluke—the following year, she placed eighth. By then, she was the world's top-ranked skater in the Women's In-line Park event. Then she got an unusual invitation: to join the world's most famous circus.

EXTREME CIRCUS

That year, Cirque du Soleil (see page 29) was putting together a winter holiday show in New York City. Called *Wintuk*, the show would feature the talents of

Aptly named: Count de Grisley was the first magician to saw a lady in half, in 1799.

extreme skateboarders, in-line skaters, and BMX bikers, along with more traditional circus acts like jugglers and acrobats. Katie joined the show and was soon performing her repertoire of tricks and stunts in a carefully choreographed spectacle involving dozens of athletes and acrobats weaving in and out of each other's way across a massive 100-foot-wide stage.

LIFE IN THE CIRQUE

How does Ketchum describe her circus experience? "Crazy! I never understood how circuses worked and all the amazing things involved. I was able to learn new skills like trapeze, jumping on stilts, and clowning." She liked it so much that she just finished her fourth year performing in *Wintuk*. Katie says she is paid very well and she gets health insurance—which comes in handy in such a hazardous sport. Best of all, joining the circus has given Katie a new way to keep doing what she loves most: skating.

WHAT AM I?

Time to give your brain a fun workout with these classic riddles. (Answers on the next page.)

1. I always tell the truth. I show off everything that I see. I come in all shapes and sizes. So tell me, what must I be?

2. Here on Earth, it is always true that a day follows a day. But there is a place where yesterday always follows today. What am I?

3. I am colorless and weightless. But if you put me in a barrel of water, the barrel will become lighter. What am I?

4. I have not flesh nor feathers, nor scales nor bone; but I do have fingers and a thumb of my own. What am I?

5. I start with "t," end with "t," and can be filled with "t." What am I?

6. Forward I am heavy, but backward I am not. What am I?

7. I have cities without houses, rivers without water, and forests without trees. What am I?

8. I am pronounced as one letter but written with three. Two different letters there are and two only in me. I am double, I am single; I am brown, blue, green, or gray. I'm read from both ends and the same either way. What am I?

9. I spend half my life dying, but live the rest. I dance without music, and breathe without breath. What am I?

10. I can sizzle like bacon, and I am made with an egg. I have plenty of backbone, but lack a good leg. I peel layers like onions, but still remain whole. I can be long like a flagpole, yet fit in a hole. What am I?

11. Though an illusion, I occur most every night. I am the familiar storyteller most often bringing tales of delight, but sometimes I may visit with stories of fright. What am I?

Answers: 1. A mirror; 2. A dictionary; 3. A hole; 4. A glove; 5. A teapot; 6. A ton; 7. A map; 8. Eye; 9. A tree; 10. A snake. 11. A dream.

Grace O'Malley, known as the "Pirate Queen," once met Queen Elizabeth I…and refused to bow.

GUNS AND ROSES

In the classic musical Annie Get Your Gun, *Annie Oakley sings, "You can't get a man with a gun." But in fact, the* real *Annie did just that—and, while she was at it, built herself a legendary career.*

LITTLE GIRL WITH A BIG GUN

Annie Oakley was a shooting star. While other little girls in Darke County, Ohio, in the 1860s were learning to cook, clean, and darn socks, Phoebe Ann Mosey (her real name) was learning to fire her dad's shotgun. By the time she was 12, she impressed local hunters by shooting the head off a running quail—an important skill that kept the meat clean of tooth-breaking buckshot. Soon Annie was supporting her widowed mother and five siblings with her shooting skills, providing game to markets and restaurants all over Darke County. Those talents would serve her well for the rest of her life.

SHOTGUN WEDDING

Oakley was 21 when she challenged celebrity marksman Frank Butler to a shooting match...and beat him. The famous sharpshooter was so taken by the five-foot-tall crack shot that he fell head over heels in love with her. They were married on June 20, 1882, and Frank quickly introduced his new bride to show business. She took the stage name Annie Oakley (after her mother's father), and together they joined Buffalo Bill's traveling Wild

West Show, a touring company of trick riders, actors, and Native Americans who wowed audiences around the world. "Little Sure Shot," as Oakley was affectionately called by fellow performer Sitting Bull, could shoot the flames off a spinning wheel of candles, shatter glass balls from the back of a galloping horse, and split a playing card held edge-on with a .22 caliber rifle from 30 feet away. Her specialty was shooting the ashes off a cigarette held in the teeth of a nervous volunteer. The king of Senegal was so impressed by her marksmanship that he offered to buy her for 100,000 francs—because lions had overrun his country and he needed a sharpshooter to get rid of them. Oakley told him she appreciated the offer, but politely refused.

STRAIGHT SHOOTERS

Annie Oakley and Frank Butler were married for 44 years but never had children. Oakley loved kids, however, and thought it was especially important for girls to know how to take care of themselves. So over the years, she offered shooting lessons to girls for sport and self-defense. When the United States entered World War I in 1918, Oakley told President Woodrow Wilson that she would happily raise an army of female sharpshooters to join the fight, though he declined the offer. A terrible car accident in 1922 left her with her leg in a brace, and her health shattered. She died in 1926 at the age of 66. Frank Butler was so heartbroken at the prospect of life without her that he stopped eating. He died 18 days later.

Throughout her career, Annie Oakley taught more than 15,000 women how to use a gun.

9-CARD MAGIC TRICK

No sleight of hand is needed—it works every time (as long as you follow the instructions).

WHAT YOU NEED...

1. A standard deck of cards
2. A friend or an audience (how brave a magician are you?)
3. A table

...AND HOW TO DO IT

1. Have a friend pull nine random cards from the deck. Set the rest of the cards aside; you won't need them.
2. Shuffle the nine cards and fan them out, face down.
3. Ask your friend to pick one, memorize it, and return it to the fan. (No peeking.)
4. Reshuffle the nine cards and deal them face up, one at a time, into three stacks by dealing one to your left, one in front of you, and one to your right, then going back to the left and repeating until you've dealt out all nine cards. (See diagram on next page.) *Always* deal the cards from your left to your right. Fan each stack slightly so your friend can see the cards.
5. Ask your friend to point to the stack that has her card.
6. Pick up the stacks so that the one with your friend's

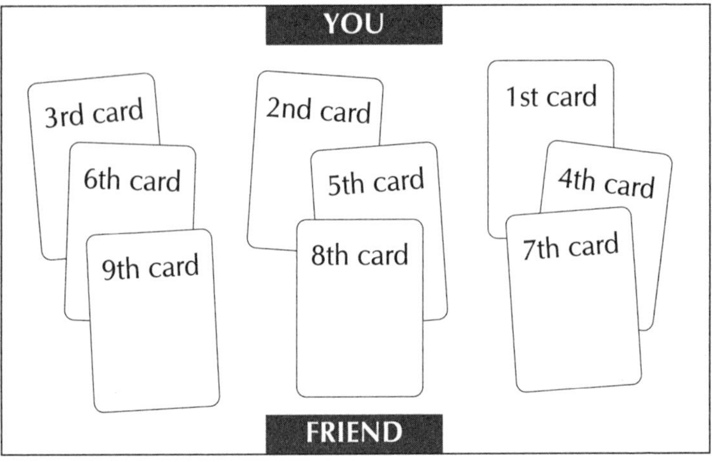

card is the second one you pick up. For example, if her card is in the left stack, pick up the middle stack first, add the stack with her card, and finally add the remaining stack.

7. Deal the nine cards face up into three stacks again, just as you did in step 4. Remember—deal from your left to your right.
8. Again, ask your friend to point to the stack with her card.
9. Pick up the stacks one last time, again making sure that the stack with your friend's card is in the middle. So if she said her card is in the far right row, you'll pick up the left stack, then add the right stack, and finally add the middle stack.
10. Throw the cards face down on the table, one at a time. Do this with dramatic flair. After you throw down the fifth card, turn it over—it will be her secret card. Ta-da!

Top-grossing animated movie of all time: *Shrek 2* has earned $919 million since its release.

A TAYLOR SWIFT TIMELINE

On December 13, 1989, Taylor Alison Swift entered the world with a song in her heart and a plan for her life. Okay, maybe she didn't get quite that early a start on her music career, but the precocious songstress kept her eye on her goals from a young age…and became one of music's top stars before she turned 21.

Age 1–5: Taylor grows up on a Christmas tree farm in Wyomissing, Pennsylvania. She loves riding ponies and building forts in the hayloft.

Age 6: Taylor discovers country music and starts singing along with recordings of Patsy Cline, the Dixie Chicks, and Shania Twain. She comes by her talent naturally: Her grandma is an opera singer.

Age 8: Taylor gets her first guitar, but it's too big for her little fingers. Meanwhile, a local children's theater director advises her to pursue a singing career.

Age 10: Taylor performs locally at karaoke contests, festivals, and county fairs. One day, a computer repairman shows her how to play three chords on her guitar. Taylor writes her first song, "Lucky You."

Age 11: Taylor sings the national anthem at a Philadelphia 76ers game. She's immediately snubbed by her friends at Wyomissing's middle school, which she says

First thing Taylor Swift did on her 18th birthday: Registered to vote, online, in her pajamas.

affected her deeply and inspired many of her songs, including "The Best Day."

Age 11½: Taylor takes her first trip to Nashville. While her mom and brother wait in the rental car, Taylor boldly marches into the office of every famous record label in town, hands them a demo CD, and says, "Hi, I'm Taylor. I want a record contract. Call me."

Age 12: Taylor learns to play the 12-string guitar, practicing until her fingers bleed, and begins writing songs, like "The Outside," that reflect her feelings of loneliness at school. She also spends the entire summer writing a 350-page novel (which hasn't been published).

Age 13: Taylor goes back to Nashville to sign a deal with RCA Records. She meets the woman who will become her main songwriting partner: Liz Rose, a middle-aged mom with two girls Taylor's age.

Age 14: The Swift family moves to Hendersonville, Tennessee, just outside Nashville, so Taylor can pursue her career. "I spent my days as a teenager, and after school I became a 40-year-old," she recalls. While daydreaming in her freshman math class, Taylor gets the idea for a song called "Tim McGraw."

Age 15: Taylor performs in Nashville's famous Bluebird Café, the nightspot where songwriters showcase their work. She's seen by record executive Scott Borchetta, who signs her to his new label, Big Machine.

Age 16: "Tim McGraw" is released as Taylor's first single, and it stays on the Billboard country chart for an

About half of the world's current population is under the age of 25.

impressive 35 weeks. The song is a true story about her breakup with a boyfriend who went off to college. "I wanted him to think of me when he heard [country singer] Tim McGraw's song 'Can't Tell Me Nothin'." Her first album, *Taylor Swift*, is released that fall…and it's a monster hit.

Age 18: Her follow-up album, *Fearless*, sells 500,000 copies within a week of its release.

Age 19: Taylor becomes the youngest artist ever to win the Country Music Association's highest honor, Entertainer of the Year. She also wins five American Music Awards and MTV's 2009 Best Female Video award for "You Belong to Me." But she's upstaged at the MTV/VMA Awards by Kanye West, who storms onto the stage and declares that Beyoncé should have won. In addition, she appears on an episode of her favorite TV show, *CSI*.

Age 20: At the 2010 Grammy Awards, Taylor becomes the youngest artist ever to win the coveted Album of the Year award, for *Fearless*. In addition, she wins three other Grammys—Best Country Album, Best Country Song, and Best Female Country Vocal Performance—and stars in the movie *Valentine's Day*.

Age 21: Six weeks before her 21st birthday, Taylor releases her third album, *Speak Now*, which includes breakup songs about her relationships with Taylor Lautner, Joe Jonas, and John Mayer. There's also an I-get-the-last-word song about Kanye West called "Innocent," which she sings at the 2010 MTV/VMA Awards.

Katharine Hepburn had a phobia of dirty hair and often sniffed the heads her costars.

SWIFT SAYINGS

A few nuggets of wisdom from music megastar Taylor Swift.

• "The tiniest little thing can change the course of your day, which can change the course of your year, which can change who you are."

• "In fairy tales, you meet Prince Charming and he's everything you ever wanted. And the bad guy is very easy to spot. Then you grow up and you realize that Prince Charming is not as easy to find as you thought, and the bad guy is not easy to spot; he's really funny, and he makes you laugh, and he has perfect hair."

• "I like to categorize the various levels of heartbreak, which range from level one, a simple letdown, to level ten, total heartbreak. A letdown is worth a few songs. A heartbreak is worth a few albums."

• "The lesson I've learned the most often in life is that you're always going to know more in the future than you know now."

• "To me, 'fearless' is not the absence of fear. It's not being completely unafraid. 'Fearless' is living in spite of those things that scare you to death."

EMBARRASSMENT IS...

Did you ever do something so embarrassing that you wished the Earth would open up and swallow you whole? That's what happened to these girls. (Their names have been changed to save them further humiliation.)

SEALED WITH A KISS

Delia had a crush on a waiter at a local restaurant. One day she went there to have a bite to eat, and as she was paying for the meal, she wrote her phone number on the receipt and kissed it with bright red lipstick. Then she ran out of the restaurant as fast as she could. But just as she was going out the door, she glanced back...and—splat!—ran into the doorjamb. There she was, lying on the ground in front of the door, looking up at the waiter, who'd followed her out because she'd left her lipstick on the table. (p.s.: He never called.)

TAKE IT OFF

Deborah was taking a junior lifesaving course when the really cute swim coach said he wanted to see everyone swim a couple of laps. He instructed them to line up at the edge of the pool and wait until he told them to dive in. When they were lined up, he called "Ready!" Deborah leaned toward the pool, anticipating his call of "Go!" But to her surprise, he added "Set!"...and Deborah dove early. The girl next to her called "Wait!" and

Shania Twain's real name is Eilleen Regina Edwards.

grabbed Deborah's bikini bottoms to stop her. It didn't—Deborah dove out of her bottoms and into the pool. The other girl was left holding half of a swimsuit and Deborah was half-naked in the pool.

ON YOUR MARK...GET SET...

And speaking of swimming, Caitlin was about to race in a big swim meet. Her boyfriend was in the bleachers with his best friend, ready to cheer her on. When the starting judge told the swimmers to take their marks, she stepped onto the block. When he said, "Get set," she bent into her diving crouch...and ripped a fart. It was so loud that the rest of the swimmers thought the noise was the starter's pistol and dove into the pool. When the judges realized what had happened, they called it a false start and the swimmers had to start over. The girl was so humiliated that she could barely swim...and finished dead last.

YOU GO, GIRL!

At a time when racism was rampant in the United States and blacks weren't allowed to perform on white stages in America, Josephine Baker took her revolutionary dancing act to Paris… and became an international sensation. *(For more "go girls," turn to pages 169 and 250.)*

JAZZ HOTTIE

"If you've got it, flaunt it!" could have been Josephine Baker's motto. But her beginnings were about as humble as they could have been. Born in 1906 to a single mother, Josephine was already working as a housekeeper at age eight and wound up homeless on the streets of St. Louis by age 12. But she found she could make a little money by dancing on street corners, and her talent caught the attention of entertainment scouts for vaudeville theaters. After a few years of performing in various clubs, she headed to New York to dance at a black theater in a chorus line.

Her biggest break came in 1925 when she got a chance to dance on a Paris stage…and decided to do it wearing nothing but a circle of feathers around her waist.

BLACK PEARL

Overnight, Baker's sensational dancing made her the toast of Paris and a bona fide star. Her uninhibited performances, exotic beauty, and charisma earned her nicknames like "Black Venus" and "Black Pearl." The French

The world's rarest blood type, A-H, is found in fewer than a dozen people worldwide.

had never seen anything like her: She wore her hair shellacked in pin curls that framed her big brown eyes, her lips were painted blood red, and her "barely there" costumes included strings of pearls, beads, and the showstopper of them all—a string of 16 bananas and nothing else. Men showered her with diamonds, cars, and more than 1,500 marriage proposals. By 1927 the poor little girl from St. Louis—who was once told by a white couple she worked for to "be sure not to kiss the baby"—had become the highest-paid entertainer in Europe.

LIVING LARGE

Baker lived up to her superstar image by spending lavish sums of money on clothes and keeping exotic pets, including a chimp named Ethel and pig named Albert. Magazine photos showed her strolling with her pet cheetah, Chiquita, down the Avenue des Champs-Elysées in Paris. In fact, fans could see Josephine Baker doing all kinds of things: She was the most photographed woman in the world.

Baker was married four times and adopted 12 children of different nationalities, dubbing them her "rainbow tribe." She continued to perform to packed houses her entire life, and, even though she lived in France, she was a champion of civil rights in the U.S. and appeared with Martin Luther King in 1963's March on Washington. When she died in 1975, she proved she could still bring in an audience: More than 20,000 Parisians lined the streets to watch her coffin pass by.

Most expensive movie ever produced: *Pirates of the Caribbean: At World's End* ($300 million).

EXTREME PETS

When it comes to pets, sometimes a dog or cat just isn't enough.

THE EMPRESS GOES APE

In 1808 a French naval officer brought an orangutan back from Borneo and gave it to Napoleon's wife, Empress Josephine. She kept the ape at her country home, Malmaison, outside Paris. The empress especially liked dressing her pet in a man's formal jacket and having it sit with her at the dinner table—all the more unusual because the ape was a female.

WILD COLONIAL KINGDOM

In colonial America, it wasn't unusual to see tame deer, wearing gold collars or colorful neckerchiefs, wandering around people's yards. Many colonial kids also kept pet squirrels that perched on their shoulders or skittered after them on leashes made of gold chain. One writer at the time, Edward Topsell, described the squirrels sold in the markets of many towns as "sweet sportful beasts and very pleasant playfellows in a house." Since squirrels could easily chew their way through wood, special tin cages were built to house them. Colonial tinsmiths even went so far as to design cages that looked like miniature mills with waterwheels that served as exercise wheels for the squirrels.

THIS BATHROOM'S OCCUPIED

In 1826 the Marquis de Lafayette gave President John Quincy Adams a very special gift—an alligator. Adams kept the reptile in a bathroom off the East Room of the White House, claiming he liked having it around because he enjoyed the "spectacle of guests fleeing the room in terror." He kept it for a few months before donating it to a zoo.

WHOSE LION NOW?

In 1941 actress Tallulah Bankhead bought her pet lion, Winston Churchill, as a cub from a circus in Reno, Nevada, where she was getting a divorce. The fuzzy feline accompanied her on tour while she was starring in several plays, and he even took curtain calls with her. Bankhead liked to shock friends at parties by declaring, "I take my pet lion to church every Sunday. He has to eat." Winston finally grew too large to handle safely and went to live at the Bronx Zoo.

AGENT 355

Some spies are so secretive that their identities remain unknown even after they die. Agent 355 was one of them…and she was also a woman.

SPY RING

The year was 1778. The American colonies were fighting desperately for their independence from England, and were trying every tactic they could think of to help win the war, including espionage. Secret spy rings had formed all over the colonies, helping deliver vital information to the American military. Major Benjamin Tallmadge, who was based in New York City and Long Island, assembled his own top-flight group of spies—code-named "the Culper Ring"—to supply the leader of the American troops, General George Washington, with British military secrets.

The Culper Ring became the most famous spy group of the American Revolution. They corresponded in invisible ink, wrote in secret codes, and hid packets of information in secret places to be picked up later by other agents.

MYSTERY WOMAN

The Culper Ring was always searching for clever ways to gain access to British secrets. Many of the colonists still socialized with British officers, and one officer, Major Andre, was known for his love of pretty girls. So the leader of the Ring, Abraham Woodhull, got an idea: Why not recruit a beautiful woman to be a spy? And he found the perfect one. Who was she? No one knows. To this day, all that's known about her are a few details of her life and her code name: Agent 355.

355 + 723 = LOVE

Agent 355's life as a spy wasn't all work and no play. According to some accounts of her shadowy life, she worked closely with a fellow agent named Robert Townsend (code name: Agent 723), and they eventually fell in love. But sadly, her story does not have a happy ending. Historians believe that 355's luck ran out in 1780: Betrayed by Benedict Arnold, the most famous traitor in American history, she was captured by the British and held on the prison ship *Jersey*. Soon after, while still a captive, Agent 355 died.

THE WALL

Today, at the Central Intelligence Agency's headquarters in Langley, Virginia, a memorial wall honors agents who died while serving as spies for the United States. Each agent is represented by a star chiseled into the marble wall. As of 2011, there were 102 stars. Below the stars, in a glass case, a book of honor lists the names of only 62 of the 102 agents. The names of the other 40 remain a secret—but Agent 355 is believed to be one of those secret stars.

Reticulated pythons can grow to a length of 27 feet—as long as a school bus.

THE SECRET LANGUAGE OF FLOWERS

Imagine you're living in the 1700s and are very interested in a certain person, but you don't know how to tell him how you feel. A note would be too bold. You can't text or e-mail. So what do you do? Say it with flowers.

SECRET CODE

In 1718 Lady Mary Wortley Montagu, the wife of a British ambassador, returned home to England with interesting news from her travels in Turkey. The Turks, she told her British friends, had invented a secret language, one in which you gave a person certain flowers to express your feelings of love and attraction. Different flowers signaled different emotions, she said: Purple lilacs meant the giver was feeling the first emotions of a crush. Red roses meant full-blown love. Violets meant true-blue faithfulness. If you received a flower with your right hand, you were saying "Yes!" If you used your left, that meant "Sorry, Charlie." Lady Montagu's friends were intrigued by this exotic "language"...so intrigued that they shared it with *their* friends. And "flower talk" began to spread like weeds in a garden.

TUSSIE MUSSIES

Before long, "tussie mussies," small bouquets of flowers, plants, and herbs, became all the rage in England. Men gave them to women, women gave them to men, and all were chock-full of meaning. For instance, red roses meant "love," but when put in a bouquet with baby's breath and ferns, the meaning changed to "sincere and everlasting love." Complex dictionaries were published so the giver and receiver would both know what each flower meant. Here's how one couple—we'll call them Roger and Felicity—might have communicated…just by sending bouquets to each other.

ROGER'S BOUQUET TO FELICITY

Yellow acacia: "secret love"

Coreopsis: "love at first sight"

Ranunculus: "I am dazzled by your charms."

Yellow jasmine: "grace and elegance"

Walnut: "intellect"

Hepatica: "confidence"

Chickweed: "rendezvous"

Ivy geranium: "Your hand at the next dance."

Witch hazel: "a spell"

Veronica: "fidelity"

Peach blossom: "I am your captive."

Pomegranate: "foolishness"

Forget-me-not: "true love"

Viburnum: "I die if neglected"

(Translation)

Dear Felicity,

Although I've kept it a *secret*, it was *love at first sight* when I met you. *I'm dazzled by your charm*, *grace*, and *intelligence*. I'm *confident* you'll *rendezvous* with me *at the next dance*. I'm under your *spell* and will always be your *faithful captive. I would die if you neglected me.*

Your *true love*, Roger

FELICITY'S BOUQUET TO ROGER

Snapdragon: "presumption"

Frog orphrys: "disgust"

Rue: "disdain"

Japanese rose: "Beauty is your only attraction."

hydrangea: "You are cold."

Cup and saucer vine: "gossip"

Dogsbane: "deceit"

Onion: "unpleasantness, odor"

Lichen: "solitude"

Dragonswort: "horror"

Butterfly weed: "Let me go."

Tansy: "I declare against you."

Birdsfoot trefoil: "revenge"

Coltsfoot: "Justice shall be done."

(Translation)

Roger,

How *presumptuous* of you! Frankly, you *disgust* me. I have nothing but *disdain* for you. *All you have is your good looks*, and you're as *cold* as ice. You do nothing but *gossip* and *tell lies*. In a word—you *stink*. I'd rather *live alone* forever than endure the *horror* of being with you. *Let me go*, or I'll *declare against you*. Then I'll have my *revenge* and *justice will be done*!

Felicity

SCENT-SATIONAL

Want to work in the perfume industry? Here's a career to think about: the most important job in the business, so important that it's known by just two words—the Nose.

THE NOSE KNOWS

In a perfume factory, a person known as "the Nose," or the *perfumer*, is the heart of the company. His or her highly developed sense of smell can identify thousands of scents. The Nose is the person who develops new blends of perfumes and creates scents for products like soaps and shampoos—and has the all-important job of deciding when a perfume has reached perfection and is ready to sell.

NOSE TO THE GRINDSTONE

How do you become a Nose? First, you'll need a college degree in chemistry. Then you'll apprentice with an established Nose at a perfume company (there are about 1,000 Noses working worldwide), where you'll learn about each perfume's four key ingredients: flowers, herbs, spices, and an animal oil called *musk*. You'll also be trained to recognize a perfume's three "notes": the *top* (the first scent you smell, but the shortest-lasting), the *middle* (one that lasts a little longer), and the *base* (the one that lingers the longest). And, if you want to become one of the top Noses—there are only about 50 in the world—you'll also need to spend a few years studying in Grasse, France, the "world capital of perfume."

The best-selling perfume in the world, Chanel No. 5, is a mix of rose, jasmine, and synthetic musk.

NUMBER 7

Seven seas, seven wonders of the world...it's amazing how often the number 7 pops up in culture and science.

THE ANCIENT WORLD

- Ancient Rome and Constantinople were each built on 7 hills.
- There were 7 Wonders of the Ancient World: the Hanging Gardens of Babylon, the Temple of Artemis at Ephesus, the Statue of Zeus at Olympia, the Mausoleum of Halicarnassus, the Colossus of Rhodes, the Lighthouse of Alexandria, and the Great Pyramid at Giza. (Only the Great Pyramid remains standing.)

SCIENCE

- Most mammals have 7 vertebrae in their neck.
- According to the classification system that doctors use, there are 7 types of viruses.
- 7 objects in the solar system are easily visible to the naked eye: the sun, the moon, Mercury, Venus, Mars, Jupiter, and Saturn.

FOLKLORE

- In many folk traditions, the 7th son of a 7th son is a very special boy: In Ireland, he'll be a healer. In England, he'll have magic powers. In Latin America, he will be a werewolf.

More than half of all American homes have three or more TV sets.

- The legendary kingdom of Atlantis was said to have 7 islands.
- Many civilizations have their "Seven Seas." In medieval Europe, they were the Mediterranean, the Adriatic, the Black Sea, the Red Sea, the Indian Ocean, the Persian Gulf, and the Caspian Sea.

RELIGION

- According to the Bible's book of Genesis, the world was created in 7 days. Later, the Pharaoh of Egypt dreams of 7 years of plenty and 7 years of famine.
- A 7-branched candelabrum called a *menorah* is lit every year during the Jewish holiday of Hanukkah.
- In Islamic tradition, there are 7 heavens and 7 hells.
- Christian tradition holds that there are 7 Virtues: chastity, temperance, charity, diligence, kindness, patience, and humility. There are also 7 Deadly Sins: lust, gluttony, greed, sloth, wrath, envy, and pride.

MISCELLANEOUS

- In music, there are 7 notes in the traditional Western major scale. (The 8th note is the 1st note but in the next higher octave.)
- In his play *As You Like It,* Shakespeare wrote a famous speech describing what he called the 7 Ages of Man: the Infant, the Schoolboy, the Lover, the Soldier, the Judge, the Old Man, and Death.

In 1897 circus star Lena Jordan became the first person to do a triple somersault on the trapeze.

WHAT AM I?

More classic riddles to sharpen your wits.

1. I come once in a minute, twice in a moment, but never in a thousand years. What am I?

2. The more you have of me, the less you see. What am I?

3. I have an eye that is neither blue nor green nor brown nor gray. I cannot blink, nor can I see. But I am stronger and faster than any man alive. What am I?

4. I have a head and a tail and I am brown. I can roll, spin, and bounce on the ground. No legs have I, but it's easy for me to travel around. What am I?

5. My life is measured in hours. I serve by being devoured. Thin, I am quick. Fat, I am slow. Often seen on cakes and sometimes at wakes. The wind is my foe. What am I?

6. I am a coat that can only be put on when wet. What am I?

Answers: 1. The letter M; 2. Darkness; 3. A hurricane; 4. A penny; 5. A candle; 6. Paint.

One volcano in Italy has been erupting nonstop for 2,000 years.

IT'S GREEK TO ME!

When the Romans adopted the gods worshipped by the ancient Greeks, they gave them new Latin names. Can you match each Greek goddess with her Roman counterpart?

GREEK

1. Athena, goddess of war, wisdom, and domestic crafts
2. Aphrodite, goddess of love and beauty
3. Artemis, goddess of the hunt, nature, and birth
4. Demeter, goddess of the harvest
5. Eos, goddess of the dawn
6. Hera, goddess of marriage
7. Hestia, goddess of the hearth and home
8. Tyche, goddess of chance and prosperity
9. Nike, goddess of victory
10. Persephone, goddess of the underworld

ROMAN

a. Aurora

b. Victoria

c. Fortuna

d. Minerva

e. Juno

f. Vesta

g. Proserpina

h. Venus

i. Diana

j. Ceres

ANSWERS: 1–d; 2–h; 3–i; 4–j; 5–a; 6–e; 7–f; 8–c; 9–b; 10–g.

First female airline pilot: Emily Warner was hired by Frontier Airlines in 1973.

RECIPE FOR BEAUTY

Why spend a gazillion dollars buying beauty products when you can whip up your own?

ROSE WATER FACIAL TONER

Spray or pat this refreshing tonic on your face after exercising or whenever your skin feels oily.

Ingredients

½ cup distilled witch hazel

½ cup rose water (see instructions below)*

¾ teaspoon vegetable glycerin

Directions

1. Combine witch hazel, glycerin, and rose water, and pour into a small spray bottle.
2. Shake before each use.

*To Make Rose Water

1. Pick one cup of rose petals as early in the morning as you can.
2. Place the petals in a colander and rinse in cool water to remove dirt and insects.
3. Transfer the clean petals to a pot. Add two cups of boiling water.
4. Cover and let stand until the liquid has cooled.
5. Remove rose petals by straining, and pour rose water into a clean glass jar.
6. Store in refrigerator.

The tapir, a small mammal related to horses, has 14 toes: 4 on each front foot, 3 on each back foot.

BODY DOUBLE

When you're watching a movie, it's easy to think that an actress is perfect—beautiful and talented. But in truth, what you're seeing might not be her at all—because some part of her body is actually being played by a different actor!

IT'S ONLY MAKE-BELIEVE

The film industry is all about making what's *not* real seem real. And like everything else in the movies, an actresses isn't always what she seems to be. She might not feel comfortable showing certain parts of her body on camera. Or a role might require her to play the piano, which she can't actually do. When that happens, producers often bring in a "body double"—an actress who makes an entire career out of substituting for other actresses. Sometimes the double does a "head-to-toe" shot with her face turned away from the camera, wearing a wig that exactly matches the star's hair. Other times, she just "stands in" for someone's hands, legs, or torso. The "real" actress (or actor—they have body doubles, too) then does all her own close-ups. Many of these body doubles also work as stuntwomen (and men).

Here are actresses who make their living…being somebody else's body.

ACTRESS: Kate Clarke

DOUBLES FOR: Angelina Jolie and Kate Beckinsale

Kate Clarke has worked as a body double for some of the

most beautiful women in the world. This 5'8" brunette also works as a stand-in for lead actresses on movie sets, doing test runs of lines and scenes while the film crew adjusts the lighting. As a body double, she knows she has to stay in tip-top shape—she eats right and does Pilates, yoga, and weightlifting. Besides being a stand-in and body double, Clarke is also a screenwriter. She says her mother never understood her desire to move to Los Angeles. "She told me normal people don't do that. Now she thinks it's great."

ACTRESSES: Ballet dancers Kimberly Prosa and Sarah Lane
DOUBLES FOR:
Natalie Portman

Natalie Portman is an accomplished actress, but even after a year of grueling ballet classes five hours a day, she needed help pulling off her prima ballerina role in the 2010 film *Black Swan*. Look closely—it's Portman from the waist up, but she's not actually doing most of the dancing. Ballet dancer Kimberly Prosa showed up to audition as an extra

...was inducted into the National Cowgirl Hall of Fame.

in the film and ended up as one of Portman's body doubles when director Darren Aronofsky pulled her aside and told her that she looked a lot like Portman. Prosa was thrilled to step in. "They were shooting me from the waist down. I did stunt doubling as well, fight scenes and getting pushed through mirrors," she told one interviewer. Producers enlisted a second dancer—Sarah Lane, a soloist with American Ballet Theater—to double for Portman in the technically demanding *fouéttes* (kicking one leg out while turning on the other leg) and *pointe* work (dancing on the tips of the toes). And those gnarly, disfigured feet in one scene? They're Kimberly Prosa's...with a lot of special-effects makeup.

ACTRESS: Alisa Hensley
DOUBLES FOR: Cameron Diaz, Charlize Theron, and Nicole Kidman

Hensley grew up in a circus family and went into show business as a stunt double and body double. Nearly six feet tall, this blonde actress often doubles for other tall blondes. But she has more skills than that—she holds a black belt in tae kwon do, knows how to use firearms (and a bullwhip), and she's comfortable rappelling down mountains, jet skiing, doing tricks on a trampoline, and zooming around on a motorcycle. *Muscle & Fitness* magazine named her one of the "20 Most Fit Women of All Time." No wonder actresses want her body to be *their* body!

The English National Ballet goes through about 3,500 pairs of pointe shoes per year.

MAISIE FROM JERSEY

Next up in our "real-girl" interviews: Maisie, a 13-year-old who lives in New Jersey. She's totally obsessed with food and cooking, and she even has her own cooking website. Here are some more facts about Maisie…then try out her yummy s'mores cupcake recipe on the next page!

- **Passion:** The Food Network's *Cake Boss, Iron Chef,* and *Chopped.* (I told you I was obsessed with cooking.) I also like to check out kids' cooking videos on YouTube.
- **Collecting:** I have an astonishingly large collection of cookbooks, from kid stuff to Williams-Sonoma and Alice Waters. I also love to collect catalogs.
- **Favorite website:** I visit IMDb a lot. That's where I find out about my current fave celebs like Emma Roberts, Anne Hathaway, Jaden Smith, and Emma Watson.
- **My reading list:** I love the Harry Potter series. My new interest is sci-fi like *The Illustrated Man* by Ray Bradbury. I'm currently reading *We Beat the Street* by Sampson Davis, George Jenkins, and Rameck Hunt. I also like books about unusual facts, like *Guinness World Records, Ripley's Believe It or Not,* and *Uncle John's Bathroom Readers* (really).
- **Music:** I'm pretty much into Hot 100–type songs by artists like Bruno Mars and B.o.B.
- **Movies:** *Valentine's Day, Tron Legacy,* and all of the Harry Potter movies.
- **For fun:** I like magic tricks—sleight of hand, cards, you name it.
- **My other not-so-secret obsession:** The musical *Billy Elliot.* I've seen it three times, taken the backstage tour, and collected six autographs...and I can tell you the name of every actor who's played Billy in New York.

In Australia, underpants are called "Reg Grundys" (rhymes with "undies").

S'MORES CUPCAKES

Leave your marshmallow-roasting stick at the door—you can make these s'mores in the kitchen.

Servings: 18

Time: 60 minutes

SUPPLIES

- Measuring spoons and cups
- Mixing bowls
- Cupcake pan and paper liners
- Electric mixer

MAKING THE CUPCAKES

Ingredients:

- 1 package yellow cake mix
- 1⅓ cups water
- 3 eggs
- ⅓ cup vegetable oil
- ½ teaspoon vanilla
- 1 cup chocolate-covered graham crackers (about 12), chopped into large pieces

Before You Begin:

- Preheat the oven to 350 degrees.
- Line the cupcake pan with the paper liners.

Directions:

1. In a large mixing bowl, combine the cake mix, water, eggs, oil, and vanilla.
2. With your mixer at medium-low speed, beat the batter until well mixed.

3. Turn the mixer up to medium-high speed and beat for 2 more minutes.
4. Stir in the chopped graham crackers.
5. Divide the batter among cupcake liners.
6. Bake for 15–18 minutes, or until a toothpick inserted into the center comes out clean.
7. Cool 10 minutes in pan and then transfer the cupcakes to racks to cool completely.

MAKING THE FROSTING

Ingredients:

- 1 (7-ounce) jar of marshmallow cream
- ½ cup butter, at room temperature
- 2 cups powdered sugar
- 1–2 teaspoons milk
- 18 Teddy Grahams honey graham snacks and broken chocolate bars

Directions:

1. Heat the marshmallow cream in the microwave for 15–20 seconds.
2. Transfer the warm marshmallow cream into a large mixing bowl.
3. Add the butter and powdered sugar and beat at medium speed.
4. Starting with ½ teaspoon at a time, add enough milk until marshmallow frosting becomes spreadable.
5. Frost the cupcakes and decorate each with a Teddy Graham and pieces of broken chocolate.

Juliette Gordon Low, founder of the Girl Scouts, was buried in her Girl Scout uniform.

ALL ABOUT ME

Here's what a few Hollywood stars have to say about themselves.

"I was the editor of the school newspaper and in drama club and choir, so I was not a popular girl in the traditional sense, but I think I was known for being relatively scathing."

—**Tina Fey**

"When other little girls wanted to be ballet dancers, I kind of wanted to be a vampire."

—**Angelina Jolie**

"I'm a pretty girl who's a model who doesn't suck as an actress."

—**Cameron Diaz**

"I'm not homely enough to play the nerdy girl and not nearly pretty enough to play the pretty girl."

—**Kristen Bell**

"If I showed you scripts from my first few movies, the descriptions of my characters all said 'the ugly girl.'"

—**Winona Ryder**

"I'm not that girl from *Freaky Friday* anymore! I'm a real adult. In fact, I hate children! I hate them all!"

—**Lindsay Lohan**

"I'm cute—and God, I hate that. Because that's not cool. I'm like your niece, and nobody wants to date their niece. It's the chubby cheeks. The whole reason people voted for me on *American Idol* is because I'm an everyday, normal girl."

—**Kelly Clarkson**

THE NAME GAME

Ever thought about what you might name your kids? Here are some people who had some, uh, unusual ideas about that.

HERE, PRINCE!

When choosing a child's name, some parents pick a first name that goes perfectly with their last name, like Texas governor Jim Hogg, who named his daughter Ima (her name is Ima Hogg); or actor Rob Morrow, who named his daughter Tu (Tu Morrow).

Superstar Michael Jackson really took his "King of Pop" title to heart and named one son Michael Jr. but called him Prince, and named the other Prince Michael II. Michael's brother Jermaine also took the royal approach and named his son Jermajesty.

There are parents who believe that an extraordinary name will make their children extraordinary, like magician Penn Jillette, who named his daughter Moxie CrimeFighter, and Nicolas Cage, who chose Superman's birth name, Kal-El, for his son.

MINAME S. WEIRD

And let's not forget parents who are weird for weird's sake, like the mom and dad in China who wanted to name their daughter @, or the parents from New Zealand who cursed their daughter by naming her Talula Does The Hula In Hawaii. (She went to court at age nine and got *that* changed.)

Ripley's Believe It or Not museum has a portrait of rapper Eminem made out of 1,000 M&Ms.

But don't feel too sorry for kids with weird names. According to Dr. Jean Twenge of San Diego State University, parents used to give kids names that would help them fit in. But now they choose names that will help them stand out—and it works. Studies show that women with unusual first names score higher on scales of friendliness and self-acceptance than those with more common names.

*   *   *

THEY NAMED THEIR KID *WHAT*????

CELEBRITY	BABY
Shannyn Sossaman (actress)	Audio Science (boy)
Bob Geldof/Paula Yates (producer, Live Aid/TV host)	Fifi Trixibelle (girl) Peaches Honeyblossom (girl) Little Pixie (girl)
Robert Rodriguez (director)	Racer (boy) Rogue (boy) Rocket (boy) Rebel (boy)
Bono (musician)	Memphis Eve (girl)
Jamie Oliver/Jools Oliver (chef/model)	Poppy Honey (girl) Daisy Boo (girl) Petal Blossom Rainbow (girl) Buddy Bear (boy)
Jason Lee (actor)	Pilot Inspektor (boy)
Erykah Badu (musician)	Seven (boy) Puma (girl) Mars (girl)

BLOOPERS

Every movie has 'em. Here are some recent "oops!" moments from Hollywood.

The *Twilight* movies

Story: Human Bella Swan (Kristen Stewart) must chose between her love for vampire Edward Cullen (Robert Pattinson) and her best friend, werewolf Jacob Black (Taylor Lautner).

- In *Twilight* (2008), when Edward and Bella have a conversation in the woods, Bella drops her backpack in front of a tree. In the next shot, the pack is gone.
- In the *Twilight* scene where Edward reveals his identity to Bella, the epaulet on his jacket changes back and forth from buttoned to unbuttoned.
- After the final battle scene in *Eclipse* (2010), when Jacob transforms from werewolf to human, you can see he's wearing a pair of flesh-colored boxers.

Harry Potter and the Deathly Hallows: Part 1 (2010)

Story: Harry Potter (Daniel Radcliffe) and his friends Ron (Rupert Grint) and Hermione (Emma Watson) set out to find and destroy the horcruxes of Lord Voldemort (Ralph Fiennes).

- When Harry shows the house-elf Kreacher a locket belonging to Regulus Black, the chain is latched together. In the next shot, it's detached.

- When the death-eater Yaxley reprimands Reg Cattermole (Ron Weasley in disguise) at the Ministry of Magic, the letter M on Yaxley's tie pin shifts from left to right.
- Several mistakes happen while Xenophilius Lovegood (Rhys Ifans) draws the symbols for the Deathly Hallows (a straight line for the Elder Wand, a circle for the Resurrection Stone, and a triangle for the Invisibility Cape). First there's a smudge on the parchment, which is gone by the end of the scene. And when Xenophilius first draws the Elder Wand symbol, he has it touch the bottom of the circle. But moments later, when he draws the triangle, the line no longer touches the circle.

Avatar (2009)

Story: Jake Sully, a paraplegic marine, must make a life-and-death choice between following his commander's orders or protecting the planet Pandora.

- When Jake (Sam Worthington) lands on Pandora in the transport shuttle, he lifts his legs into his wheelchair with his hands and puts them in place. Later in the scene, he moves his left leg without using his hands.
- At the beginning of the movie, when the transport shuttle has landed and the doors are open, you can see an extra in the background having trouble with his breathing mask—it keeps slipping off, but he never suffers the fatal consequence of inhaling Pandora's atmosphere.

HERE COMES THE BRIDE

There's more to a wedding than just a cake and a big white dress. There's something borrowed, something blue...and a bunch of other weird things. Where did they all come from?

THE BRIDE WEARS WHITE

In Western culture, a white wedding dress has come to symbolize purity. But brides didn't always wear white; for centuries, they simply wore their best dress, regardless of color. Then, in 1840, England's Queen Victoria married Prince Albert in a shoulderless white satin-and-lace gown...and suddenly white bridal gowns were all the rage. Today, many white wedding dresses still look like they came right out of Victorian times.

SEALED WITH A KISS

We all know that no couple is *really* married until that big smooch at the end of the wedding ceremony. This ritual comes from ancient Rome, where a kiss was considered a legal bond that sealed all contracts and made them official. Without the kiss, no deal.

THE WEDDING PARTY

Ever wonder why so many people—ushers and bridesmaids, best man, maid of honor—stand at the altar with

In Japanese weddings, a pair of ducks or geese often waddles down the aisle...

the bride and groom? This tradition also comes from the ancient Romans, who believed that demons stalked the newlyweds. Bridesmaids and the rest of the wedding party were chosen to protect the new couple, and even dressed like them to confuse the evil spirits.

RICE IS NICE

Throwing grain at the newlyweds, a practice begun in ancient Egypt, is a way to wish the happy couple fertility and prosperity. In some cultures, wedding guests throw blossoms or other seed-bearing plants. Rice, which gradually became the seed of choice in the United States, suddenly fell out of favor in the 1990s amid rumors that rice was unhealthy for birds and could even make them explode. The rumor has since been debunked, but many wedding guests now throw birdseed instead.

STOMP THE GLASS

In Jewish weddings, the groom stomps on a wineglass wrapped in cloth, and all the guests yell "*Mazel tov!*" ("Good luck!" or "Congratulations!") This ritual recalls the destruction of the Holy Temple in Jerusalem by the Romans in A.D. 70, and serves to remind the couple that life is a mixture of joy and sorrow.

THE BRIDAL SHOWER

The bridal shower "gift party" started centuries ago as a backup plan in case the bride's father didn't approve of her wedding. Dad's refusal meant she would get no *dowry*—the sheets, plates, silverware, clothes, land, or cash that a bride usually brought into a marriage. In that situation, sympathetic villagers would throw the bride a party to "shower" her with the things she needed to set up a household with her new husband.

THE BRIDAL VEIL

In ancient times (and still today, in parts of Asia and the Middle East), marriages were arranged between families, and often a bride and groom met for the first time on their wedding day. The bride's family covered her face with a veil so the groom would not be able to see her face until after the ceremony, in case he didn't like what he saw and tried to make a run for it.

• Roman brides wore veils of heavy red fabric to hide them from evil spirits. In ancient Greece, the bride's protective veil was yellow.

• The white veil became popular in England in the 16th century as a symbol of modesty and chastity. It was introduced to the United States by Nelly Custis in 1799 when she married Major Lawrence Lewis, a nephew of George Washington. Major Lewis had first seen Miss Custis's face peeking out a window from behind a white lace curtain, and she wanted to re-create that moment in her wedding. So she wore a white lace veil…and started a new American fashion trend.

THE KICKOFF

In Europe in the 1300s, wedding guests hurled shoes at the newlyweds to kick bad spirits away (leather was believed to repel evil). Since the 20th century, people have tied shoes to the bumper of the newlyweds' car, along with cans and other noisemakers. Why? Not only to frighten those bad spirits away, but also to re-create the old-fashioned *shivaree* ("rough serenade"), a tradition that began in medieval France. The goal of the shivaree was for the guests to have fun…and make as much noise as possible to interrupt the couple's wedding night.

EMILY THE ECCENTRIC

With her quirky, short poems full of odd punctuation and themes of spirituality and death—and often barbed humor—Emily Dickinson (1830–86) revolutionized American poetry. And she was more than a little quirky herself. Here are 10 facts about the poet known as "the Eccentric Recluse."

1. Dickinson wrote nearly 1,800 poems in her lifetime, but no one knew about most of them. Barely a dozen were published while she was alive. The first was a valentine poem published anonymously in a local newspaper, the *Springfield Daily Republican*, on February 20, 1852.

2. After Emily died, her sister, Lavinia, found the poems hidden in Emily's room. They were written on the backs of envelopes, on wrapping paper and recipes, and stitched together into neat little booklets.

3. Emily almost always dressed in white.

4. In her 55 years, Emily left her hometown of Amherst, Massachusetts, only a few times. Once was to attend college at nearby Mount Holyoke Female Seminary, which she left within a year.

5. As she got older, she rarely left her home and, later on, her room. Some scholars now believe she may have had the anxiety disorder *agoraphobia*—the fear of being out in the open.

6. Emily enjoyed corresponding with journalists, editors, and publishers. But on the rare occasions when one of them came to visit, she wouldn't let them see her; she would speak to them from another room or shout to them from upstairs.

7. Emily often gave treats to neighborhood kids by lowering food in a basket from her second-story bedroom window. The kids would catch a glimpse of her hands or arms, but never her face.

8. Even when she was sick, she wouldn't let a doctor actually see her—he had to "examine" her from another room as she walked slowly past the open door.

9. Emily died in May 1886. For her funeral, she was dressed in white and laid out in a white coffin with flowers—violets, heliotropes, and a lady's-slipper orchid—in the coffin with her. Following her prearranged directions, her pallbearers carried the coffin in a circle around her flower garden, through a barn behind the house, and across a field of buttercups to Amherst's West Cemetery.

10. Her grave is marked with a marble slab engraved with the final words Dickinson wrote in a letter to her cousins shortly before she died—"Called Back."

SECRET INGREDIENTS

In ancient Rome, women used everything from ground oyster shells to sheep sweat in their cosmetics. But if you think nobody puts weird things in makeup anymore, have a look at these ingredients that are still used today—sometimes hidden behind very scientific names.

Ingredient: Fish scales
Found in: Nail polish, lip gloss, shampoo
Why: Fish scales are made up mostly of *guanine*, an amino acid that gives them a pearly, iridescent look. Cosmetic companies use guanine (often called Pearl Essence, Dew Pearl, or Mearlmaid) to make your lips shine, nails sparkle, and hair glow.

Ingredient: Diamond dust
Found in: Nail polish, skin peels, blush
Why: Diamonds are the hardest natural material on Earth, so even a tiny bit of diamond dust added to nail polish makes it scratch-resistant. Diamond dust is also finer and gentler than any sandpaper, so it's often used in treatments to remove dead skin cells. And how does it look? Madonna brushes diamond dust on her cheeks to give her performance that extra sparkle.

Ingredient: Rooster combs
Found in: Wrinkle-reducing creams, joint-pain creams
Why: Rooster combs (those little floppy red things on a

rooster's head) are loaded with *hyaluronic acid*, nicknamed "HA." This substance has been called the "goo molecule" because of its lubricating qualities—it heals cell tissue and can reduce joint pain. People with achy joints often get HA shots in their knees or shoulders, and all of those healing qualities make it a much-wanted ingredient in cosmetic creams to keep skin smooth and wrinkle-resistant.

Ingredient: Snail slime

Found in: Acne cream, eye cream, facial treatments

Why: The slippery fluid secreted by snails has been found to reduce the scarring caused by acne. This substance, known scientifically as *glycoconjugate*, also smoothes wrinkles around the eyes and forehead. If you don't want to buy the snail cream, give your local salon a call and sign up for a snail-slime facial.

Ingredient: Crushed beetles

Found in: Lipstick, lip liner, eye shadow, mascara, blush

Why: Mexico's ancient Aztecs found the best source for red dye came from a little bug that lived among the spines of the prickly pear cactus. The body of the female *cochineal* beetle, when dried and ground into a fine powder, added a luscious red color to fabrics. Now, hundreds of years later, that little beetle is still used to color clothes, paints, makeup, and even fruit drinks.

Ingredient: Chili peppers

Found in: Lip plumpers, face creams, pepper spray

Why: The stuff that makes chili peppers so hot and pepper spray so effective at stopping bears or bad guys is a chemical called *capsaicin.* It's so potent that too much of it can even be deadly. However, cosmetic companies found that just the right amount of capsaicin in face creams and moisturizers plumps tissues and makes wrinkles and lines less noticeable. Some women dab it on their lips for that pouty Angelina Jolie look.

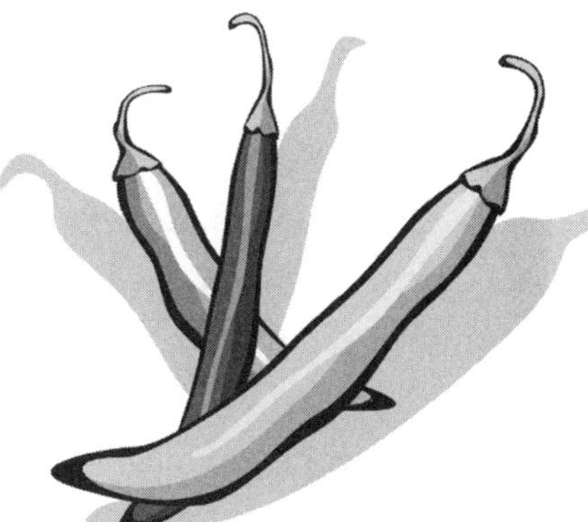

Ingredient: Fish eggs

Found in: Moisturizers, hair spray, anti-itch creams, body oils, body-firming lotions

Why: Cosmetic companies claim that fish eggs, especially caviar (from the sturgeon fish) will keep your skin and hair from drying out. Fortunately, the active ingredients—fatty acids known as *omega-3s*—are odorless.

GODDESSES RULE: ISIS

Meet the Egyptian goddess who takes care of...well, everyone.

KEEPING IT TOGETHER

In Egyptian mythology, the goddess Isis was known as "the Great Mother of the Universe." It was her job to provide water and milk for all the plants and animals on the planet from sunrise to sunset. That's why the ancient Egyptians depicted her wearing a headdress of a huge gold sun disk between two cow horns. But Isis had another special gift—she could raise the dead. When the god Set murdered Isis's husband, the god Osiris (who also happened to be her brother), he chopped up Osiris's body into 14 pieces and scattered them around the desert. The heartbroken Isis gathered up all the pieces and magically brought Osiris back to life. Their reunion lasted only long enough for them to have a son, the god Horus. Then Osiris was "promoted" to Lord of the Underworld, the land of the dead, and Isis and her husband were separated forever. The Egyptians say the great annual flooding of the Nile stems from the tears Isis sheds as she mourns for her lost Osiris.

If you like Egyptian mythology, check out *The Egypt Game* by Zilpha Keatley Snyder—an award-winning novel about a group of kids in California who find an Egyptian statue in their neighbor's shed. The kids make an altar to Isis and create a secret game where they pretend to be Egyptian gods and goddesses. Their game leads to intrigue, magic...and even murder.

✯ STARSTRUCK, PART I ✯

Want to know your best scent, your lucky numbers, your ideal ice cream flavor…and the keys to your personality? According to the ancient theory of astrology, they're all determined by when you were born.

♈ ARIES (March 20–April 19)

Element: Fire
Ruling Planet: Mars
Gemstone: Diamond
Symbol: Ram
Scent: Peppermint
Flower: Honeysuckle
Lucky Numbers: 1, 13, 47
Ice Cream: Denali's Moose Tracks

Charge! Climb a mountain? Organize a rally? Save a rain forest? That's a yes! As the first sign in the zodiac, you're a "can-do" kind of girl. You are so full of energy and ideas, you're like a walking exclamation point. But your strong opinions sometimes get you in trouble. Pick your fights—not all battles are yours to win.

Famous Aries Women: Reese Witherspoon, Keira Knightley, Norah Jones, Lady Gaga, Maya Angelou, Mariah Carey, Sandra Day O'Connor

♉ TAURUS (April 20–May 20)

Element: Earth
Ruling Planet: Venus
Gemstone: Emerald
Symbol: Bull
Scent: Lavender
Flower: Poppy
Lucky Numbers: 4, 6, 7, 8, 22, 49
Ice Cream: Häagen-Dazs Dulce de Leche

Q: What are nighttime rainbows called? A: Moonbows.

Feeling Groovy. Taureans love luxury: Think a clawfoot tub that's overflowing with bubbles, candles all around, and gourmet chocolates just within your reach. Heaven! And you not only love your creature comforts, you also appreciate beauty. You are patient, creative, calm, and loyal. But admit it—you can also be bullheaded. Remember: change happens. Try to be more flexible.

Famous Taurus Women: Tina Fey, Kirsten Dunst, Enya, Kelly Clarkson, Charlotte Brontë, Penelope Cruz

♊ GEMINI (May 21–June 20)

Element: Air
Ruling Planet: Mercury
Gemstone: Aquamarine
Symbol: Twins
Scent: Jasmine
Flower: Lily of the Valley
Lucky Numbers: 2, 3, 8, 12
Ice Cream: Ben and Jerry's Chunky Monkey

Ms. Social Butterfly. Geminis have the gift of gab. You tell the best ghost stories at slumber parties and have the best gossip in the lunchroom (even if you sometimes stretch the truth). You are charming, smart, and outgoing one minute...but you can be withdrawn and distant the next. That comes from being born under the sign of the twins. Don't worry—your charm wins out in the end.

Famous Gemini Women: Venus Williams, Mary-Kate and Ashley Olsen, Angelina Jolie, Anne Frank, Marilyn Monroe

In 19th-century England, it was considered bad manners to hold an umbrella under your arm.

♋ CANCER (June 21–July 21)

Element: Water
Ruling "Planet": The moon
Gemstone: Pearl
Symbol: Crab
Scent: Rose

Flower: White Rose
Lucky Numbers: 2, 5, 9, 12, 48
Ice Cream: Häagen-Dazs Midnight Cookies and Cream

All You Need Is Love... Cancer girls are all about family and friends. If someone has a problem, you're there first with a warm hug and a plate of fresh cookies. As bighearted as you are, you are no pushover. Being governed by the moon and the water, you can seem downright moody sometimes. Find some time to center yourself each day.

Famous Cancer Women: Meryl Streep, Missy Elliott, Selma Blair, Fantasia, Alice Munro

♌ LEO (July 22–August 21)

Element: Fire
Ruling "Planet": The sun
Gemstone: Amber
Symbol: Lion
Scent: Fennel

Flower: Sunflower
Lucky Numbers: 1, 3, 9, 93
Ice Cream: Ben & Jerry's New York Super Fudge Chunk

Roar! Living large and loving every second of it—that's you, Ms. Leo! You have the talent and presence to take center stage...and keep it. And even though you may look fierce with your wild mane of hair (Leo girls tend to have big hair), all you really want is a little r-e-s-p-e-c-t. If you don't get it, look out—a pouting, grumbling lion may appear. But you don't suffer long. Leo girls are fun.

Famous Leo Women: Jennifer Lopez, J. K. Rowling, Madonna, Halle Berry, Connie Chung, Amy Adams

♍ VIRGO: August 22–September 22

Element: Earth

Ruling Planet: Mercury

Gemstone: Topaz

Symbol: The Virgin

Scent: Jasmine

Flower: Buttercup

Lucky Numbers: 3, 4, 8, 10, 33

Ice Cream: Ben & Jerry's Maple Blondie

Be Prepared. Whether you're planning the party or taking charge of the first-aid kit, you, Virgo girl, have got it together. Your analytical nature makes you a great shopping buddy: You know where the best stores are and who has the best sales. Your room is clean, your bookshelves are organized, and you have the most recent must-read magazines on your bedside table. So what's the problem? It's impossible to be perfect all the time. Chillax.

Famous Virgo Women: Beyoncé, Salma Hayek, Nicole Richie, Fiona Apple, Mary Shelley, Mother Teresa

Don't see your sign here? Turn to page 257 for more "starstruck" astrology!

RECIPE FOR BEAUTY

Here's another do-it-yourself beauty product… perfect for relaxing after a busy day.

AROMA THERAPY BATH SALTS

Epsom salt and sea salt are well-known folk remedies for sore, achy muscles, and will make your skin feel soft and silky. After a long day at school, soak in the warm water and inhale the delicious aroma of essential oils. It's the perfect way to relax.

Ingredients

- 4 cups Epsom salt
- 2 cups sea salt
- ¾ cup baking soda
- 25 drops lavender essential oil
- 25 drops lemon essential oil
- 15 drops orange essential oil
- 15 drops peppermint essential oil

Instructions

1. Mix all of the above ingredients in a jar with a tight-fitting lid.
2. Pour one cup into your bath while the water is running.

FUNDERWEAR QUIZ

Think you know your underwear? Let's find out. Match the question on the top with the correct answer on the bottom.

1. What did most women wear under their petticoats (a loose undergarment similar to a slip) from the Middle Ages to the 1800s?

2. Men in the 1500s wore baggy shorts under their tunics. What were they called?

3. In the 1700s, wide hips were a sign of wealth. (Bigger hips meant better food.) What undergarment looked like ironing boards sticking out of a woman's sides?

4. Women in the early 1900s wore what knee-length underpants with lace on the hems?

5. What did Victorian women call underwear?

6. What did women in the 19th century wear to make their bottoms look huge?

7. In the 1890s, what baggy pants were invented so women could ride bicycles without getting their skirts caught in the spokes?

8. In the 1940s, women began making what undergarments out of silk parachute material?

A. Panties
B. Bloomers
C. *Panniers* (pan-yay)
D. "Unmentionables"

E. Drawers
F. Nothing
G. Knickerbockers
H. Bustle

ANSWERS: 1-F; 2-E; 3-C; 4-B; 5-D; 6-H; 7-G; 8-A.

IT WAS A DARK AND STORMY NIGHT

Here's a famous monster that didn't come from a comic book or a movie—it rose from the imagination of a teenage author...more than 180 years ago.

A NOVEL IDEA

Lightning flashed outside the sprawling mansion on Lake Geneva as rain pelted the windows. It was the summer of 1816, and poet Percy Bysshe Shelley and his fiancée, 19-year-old Mary Wollstonecraft Godwin, were on vacation in Switzerland. They hadn't seen the sun since their arrival, and they were going stir-crazy.

On this particular night, Mary and Percy were staying with their neighbor, fellow poet Lord Byron, and a friend named Dr. John Polidori. As the storm raged outside, they entertained each other by reading ghost stories aloud.

Then Byron closed his book and said, "I have an idea. We shall each write a ghost story." They agreed to go off to their rooms and see who could write the most frightening tale.

WRITER'S BLOCK

The storm raged on. They all worked at their stories, but it was harder that they thought. Because they were all used to writing poetry, horror stories didn't come naturally. That night, Mary tossed and turned in her sleep. She was determined to come up with the best story—one that "would speak to the mysterious fears of our nature and awaken thrilling horror." But she couldn't think of anything.

The next morning, the group shared their results. Byron had written part of a story about a man who returns from the dead. Percy's story, they all agreed, wasn't very good. Dr. Polidori's tale was a genuine spine-tingler about "a jaded, charismatic nobleman who must feed upon the blood of the living." (Years later, Polidori's story, "The Vampyre," would evolve into the Dracula legend.)

Mary was the only one who hadn't come up with anything. Days passed. Every morning her companions asked, "Have you thought of a story?" And each morning she was forced to reply "No."

A FLASH OF INSPIRATION

One evening Mary sat by the fireplace, listening to Percy and Byron talk about the possibility of reanimating a corpse with electricity. The discussion ended well after midnight, and Percy went off to bed. But Mary couldn't sleep.

"When I placed my head upon the pillow," she recalled, "I did not sleep, nor could I think." In her imagination, she pictured a pale young man kneeling beside a strange device he had built. The hideous shape of a dead body was stretched out on an operating table before him. Then she saw the corpse—under the power of some strange engine—jerk and shudder back to life. This "horrid thing" then stood up and looked at its creator with "yellow, watery eyes."

Mary sat up in terror. She looked around the room to make sure she'd only been imagining, but she couldn't shake the image of the hideous creature. That was when she realized her vision was, in fact, the story she'd been searching for.

"I have found it," she thought. "What terrified me will terrify others; and I need only describe the specter which haunted my midnight pillow." The next day, Mary announced to the group that she had finally thought of a story. She called it *Frankenstein*.

THE HORROR CONTINUES

The first version Mary wrote was just a short story, but after she and Percy were married, he encouraged her to develop it further. She eventually turned it into a novel, which was published anonymously in three parts (standard practice at the time) in 1818.

"Mary Shelley," notes one modern critic, "did not think it important enough to sign her name to the book. And since her husband wrote its preface, people assumed he had written the rest of the book as well. It was not until a later edition that the book was revealed as the work of a young girl."

The novel found an enthusiastic audience, but it wasn't enough to make Mary and Percy Shelley rich. They lived in relative poverty for most of their lives, though both published several books and many poems. Percy tragically drowned at just 29 years old, and Mary Shelley died in 1851 at the age of 53.

CREATURE FEATURES

In the 1900s, *Frankenstein* found a whole new audience, thanks to dozens of film versions. You've probably heard of the famous ones. Here are a few of the wackier ones:

I Was a Teenage Frankenstein (1957)
Frankenstein Meets the Space Monster (1965)
Jesse James Meets Frankenstein's Daughter (1966)
The Rocky Horror Picture Show (1975)
Frankenstein's Great Aunt Tillie (1984)
Frankenstein's Castle of Freaks (1974)
Frankenstein General Hospital (1988)

What do hay, tomato leaves, and carrot seeds have in common? All are used in making perfume.

KILLER MAKEUP

Today there are entire lines of cosmetics designed to help your skin appear flawless, make your eyes sparkle, and turn your lips a kissable red. But what did women do before MAC and Urban Decay?

SOLIMAN'S WATER (16th-century Europe)
What it did: This "must-have" skin lotion removed freckles, spots, and warts.

Key ingredient: Mercury

Big problem: It didn't just remove your outer layer of skin; it also destroyed the skin underneath. What's more, the mercury could make your teeth fall out and your gums recede, and if you got enough of it in your system, you went insane.

BELLADONNA (17th-century Europe)

What it did: Italian for "beautiful woman," belladonna drops were used to dilate the pupils, giving you dark, sparkling eyes.

Key ingredient: Belladonna, a poisonous plant also known as deadly nightshade

Big problem: Using too much of it caused convulsions, delirium, glaucoma, and blindness.

RED FUCUS (ancient Egypt and Rome)

What it did: A paste made from this algae made cheeks rosy and lips bright red.

Key ingredient: Red mercuric sulfide

Big problem: Mercury again! No teeth, no gums, no sanity.

DIE, DIE, MY DARLING

In the mid-1600s, an Italian woman named Giulia Toffana invented a special concoction called "Acqua Toffana" that she marketed as a cosmetic—but which was actually a poison laced with arsenic and lead. For several years, women who found themselves trapped in bad marriages sought her out, bought a vial of Acqua Toffana from her, and then quietly put it in their husbands' food. By the time authorities caught onto her, Toffana had helped more than 600 Italian women poison their husbands. She'd become so popular that some of her customers tried to hide her from the police, but in 1659 she was arrested and executed.

One billionth of a trillionth of a second is called a *zeptosecond.*

YOU GO, GIRL!

"Well-behaved women rarely make history," wrote historian Laurel Thatcher Ulrich. Check out the story of Aphra Behn, a 17th-century rabble-rouser who shook up the world. (Read about more "go girls" on pages 121 and 250.)

AUTHOR...AND SNOOP

Aphra Behn (1640–89), one of the first women in history to become a professional writer, had a *lot* to write about. From an early age, her life played out like an adventure novel. Born in England to a working-class family, Behn got a chance in her 20s to travel to a sugar colony in South America's exotic Suriname. She returned to England to marry, but when her husband suddenly died three years later, the young widow had to find some way to support herself. So what did she do? She became a spy.

AGENT 160

In 1665 war broke out between England and the Netherlands. Behn, a loyal supporter of King Charles II of England, had become friends with some members of his court. And her new friends had a request: Would she travel to Antwerp, near the Netherlands, and report back to the king with important information about the Dutch navy and the inside scoop on what was happening politically? She jumped at the chance and spied for the next year or two under the code names "Astrea" and

"Agent 160." But on her way back to England, she was involved in a terrible shipwreck. She survived, but when she returned home, she was arrested for bad debts…because the king hadn't paid her for her spy work. A friend finally paid off her debts, and Behn was released from prison in 1669.

Alone, penniless, and desperate, Behn decided to write her way out of trouble. She wrote everything—plays, poems, stories, it didn't matter…as long as they paid. And it worked: Her first play, *The Forced Marriage*, was a hit, and just like that, Aphra Behn was a professional writer. Before long she was scandalizing English society by writing openly about love and relationships. And she was equally outspoken with her friends about her own romances.

GROUNDBREAKER

In 1688 Behn published a novel called *Oroonoko, or the History of the Royal Slave*, about a doomed love between two slaves in Suriname. The book marked the first time that black people were presented sympathetically in English literature. But its publication was Behn's last hurrah. She died the next year, at age 49, and was buried in Westminster Abbey, the final resting place of British royalty and many great writers—quite an honor for a troublemaker like her.

OMENS

According to superstitious people, the universe is IM-ing you all the time—you just need to know how to read the signs. Here are a few "omens" from folklore...and what they supposedly mean.

- If you find a bird in your house, an important message will soon arrive.
- If you see an owl in daylight, you're in for some bad luck.
- If a strange dog follows you, good luck will follow, too.
- If a dog howls three times, then goes silent, someone just died.
- If you see a cat at a wedding, smile! It means good luck for the happy couple.
- If you see a white moth inside your house, beware: Death will visit soon.
- If your cat sneezes, grab your umbrella—it's going to rain.
- If you find a bee in the house, clean your room. A visitor is coming.
- If you see a spider run down its web in the afternoon, pack your bags. You're about to take a road trip.
- If you light a candle and it goes out, something wicked is lurking nearby.
- If your nose itches, expect guests. If it's the right nostril, look for a girl. The left? A boy.
- If you bite your tongue while eating, you recently told a lie. (That'll teach you!)
- If you trip going up the stairs, you'll be falling in love soon.

World's largest alphabet: Cambodian, with 74 letters.

3 THEORIES ABOUT UNLUCKY 13

Lots of people believe the number 13 is bad news. But where did the superstition come from? Here are three popular theories.

THEORY #1: The Betrayal

In the New Testament, Judas, the man who betrayed Jesus, was the last guest to sit down at the Last Supper, making it a group of 13. Thus began the saying, "If 13 people sit down at dinner together, one of them will die within the year."

THEORY #2: The Party Crasher

In Norse mythology, Loki the Troublemaker is the 13th god. Like Judas, Loki was blamed for the death of a key figure in the religion. As the story goes, when Loki was denied entrance into a gathering in Valhalla (Norse heaven), he got so angry that he crashed the party and set the wheels in motion for the death of Balder, the god of light and goodness. Loki was—you guessed it—the 13th guest at the gathering.

THEORY #3: The Friday Knights

On October 13, 1307—a Friday—King Phillip IV of France ordered the arrest, torture, and execution of every member of the Knights Templar—a sect of warrior-monks who had fought together during the Crusades and returned home to create vast estates. Why did he have them killed? He was envious of their growing power and, being monks, the Templars' first allegiance was to the church, not the king. The few who survived the purge went underground, where some say they founded a secret society that eventually became the Freemasons (as described in the book and movie *The Da Vinci Code*). From then on, "the 13th" became synonymous with very bad luck—and Friday the 13th even more so.

13-13-13-13

At precisely 13:13 (1:13 p.m.) on Friday the 13th, August 2010, 13-year-old Connor Laughlin of Carlisle, England, was struck by lightning while attending the Lowestoft Seafront Air Festival. "I was standing, holding an umbrella," he said, "and I saw the lightning coming towards me, then it just hit me. It went right through my whole body. It was like being hit by a truck, and so loud!" Luckily, he came out of it with only a small red mark on one shoulder. (Doctors say his rubber-soled shoes may have insulated him from the shock and saved his life.)

LOVE POTION NUMBER 9

This top-secret love potion was found in an old book of spells. Does it work? You be the judge.

I PUT A SPELL ON YOU

Brew this tea on a Friday as the moon is growing full, and the person you love will soon love you.

Ingredients

- 1 pinch rosemary
- 2 teaspoons black tea
- 3 pinches thyme
- 3 pinches nutmeg
- 3 fresh mint leaves
- 6 fresh rose petals
- 6 lemon leaves
- 3 cups spring water
- Sugar or honey

Instructions

Place the dry ingredients in a ceramic or copper teapot. Boil the water and add to the teapot. Let sit a few minutes, then sweeten with sugar or honey. Pour the potion into a cup and say:

Goddess of love,
Hear now my plea:
Let [beloved's name] fall in love with me!
So mote it be,
So mote it be.

Then drink the tea. On the following Friday, brew another pot of Love Potion Number 9 and give some to the person you desire. Love will soon bloom!

GODDESSES RULE: FREYJA

Meet the Norse goddess of love and beauty.

WAR AND PEACE

The Vikings, who ruled Scandinavia in the Middle Ages, believed that in the early days of the world, two tribes of gods roamed the Earth. The *Aesir*, led by a god named Odin, were rough-and-tumble hunters and fighters; the *Vanir* were a gentler race who tended the soil and made it fertile. The loveliest of the Vanir was a goddess named Freyja. Once, the Aesir challenged the Vanir to battle. A truce was called, and the Vanir surrendered Freyja as a hostage. The beautiful goddess kept peace between the two tribes.

Freyja was also known for looking after the souls of warriors who died in battle. Upon their deaths, she invited them to visit her grand hall in Asgard, the heavenly home of the Norse gods. There the fallen soldiers were given the royal treatment: wine, singing, and dancing.

Freyja married a god named Odr, and they lived happily in Asgard until, one day, Odr mysteriously disappeared. Freyja has been looking for him ever since, riding through the night in a golden chariot drawn by two gray cats. Sometimes she dons a coat made of falcon feathers and flies like a bird, always searching for her lost love. On moonless nights, Freyja's sparkling necklace of gold, silver, and diamonds can be seen high in the sky—it's what we now call the Milky Way.

CUPCAKE IN A MUG

When you need a chocolate cupcake NOW.

Servings: 1

Time: 5–10 minutes

Supplies

- 1 large microwave-safe mug
- Measuring spoons
- Microwave oven

Ingredients

- 1 can of cooking spray
- 4 tablespoons white flour
- 4 tablespoons sugar
- 4 tablespoons cocoa powder
- ¼ teaspoon baking powder
- 3 tablespoons chocolate chips
- 1 egg, beaten
- 3 tablespoons milk
- 3 tablespoons oil
- 2–3 drops of vanilla

Directions

- Spray the inside of the mug with cooking spray.
- Blend the dry ingredients in the mug.
- Add the egg to the dry ingredients and mix thoroughly.
- Add the milk and oil and mix completely.
- Add the chocolate chips and vanilla and mix again.
- Microwave for 2½ to 3 minutes.

Notes

While it's heating in the microwave, the cupcake will rise above the rim of the mug. It might even spill over the side. Don't worry—this is normal. When you take the mug out of the microwave, the cake will collapse and may look dreadful. But, as you're about to discover, looks aren't everything. Add a scoop of ice cream and dig in...delicious.

IT TAKES A WOMAN TO DO A MAN'S JOB

Not long ago, this was truly a man's world. But some women still managed to follow their dreams...by pretending to be men.

JEANNE BARÉ (1740–1803)

In 1766 the great French navigator Louis Antoine de Bougainville launched an expedition to become the first Frenchman to circle the globe. But he had no idea that one member of his crew wasn't what he appeared to be. The truth came out several months later when the ship landed in Tahiti and the local Polynesians discovered something unusual: The ship's botanist's assistant, who appeared to be a young man, was actually a woman. Twenty-six-year-old Jeanne Baré confessed that she'd joined the crew under false pretenses: She wanted to see the world and knew there was no way she could join the crew as a woman. The dumbfounded Bougainville and his crew decided to let Baré complete the voyage, and she became the first woman to go around the world. Along the way, she proved her mettle as a botanist, assisting the ship's botanist in discovering thousands of plants, one of which was named after her: a shrub they called *Baretia*. When the ship returned to France, Bougainville insisted that Baré be recognized for her invaluable contributions to the expedition. Eventually she was honored by the French government with a pension.

THE DOCTOR IS A LADY

Margaret Ann Bulkley (1792–1865) was a woman of firsts. She was the first female to earn a medical doctorate in Great Britain, graduating from the University of Edinburgh in 1812. The following year, she became the first female surgeon in the British army, and in 1826, she became the first British doctor to perform a successful Cesarean section. But she accomplished all those feats while disguised as a man and using the pseudonym of Dr. James Barry. She kept her identity secret for more than 50 years; it wasn't discovered until her death in 1865. When British military officials learned the truth, they were so concerned about a potential scandal that they sealed Dr. Barry's service records for more than 100 years. The truth about Dr. Barry—who had finished "his" military career as an inspector general of hospitals—finally came to light in 2001, when researchers found evidence that several of Margaret Ann Bulkley's relatives, including her mother, had helped her lie about her gender to get into medical school.

MR. WRITE

When she married Baron Casimir Dudevant in 1822, 19-year-old Amantine Aurore Lucile Dupin (1804–76) seemed destined for a life of wealth and privilege in 19th-century France. But marriage didn't suit the restless baroness, and in 1831, she shocked French society by leaving her husband, an act that she called "romantic rebellion." Before long, she shocked them again by doing other unladylike things, such as wearing men's clothing and smoking in public. Then she took the pen name "George Sand" and became one of the most successful novelists of her day, publishing more than 40 books and plays in her lifetime. When Dupin/Sand died, the Russian writer Ivan Turgenev said of her, "What a brave man she was, and what a good woman."

CHANGING KEYS

What do you do if your high school won't let you join the band because you're a girl? Here's one idea: Move to another state, disguise yourself as a boy, and eventually show the world by becoming a celebrated jazz musician. That's what Dorothy Tipton (1914–89) did when she left Kansas City, Missouri, for Oklahoma to begin her senior year of high school in 1933. There, she changed her name to Billy and played piano and saxophone with a number of bands. She went on to record two albums as the leader of the Billy Tipton Trio and fooled everyone for over 50 years—including several girlfriends and three adopted sons—until her death at age 74 in 1989.

*   *   *

"I learned to cook at 32. Before that, I just ate."

—chef Julia Child

BEAUTY IS IN THE EYE OF THE BEHOLDER

Pierced ears, hair extensions, tattoos—these are all body adornments that many in the Western world think are attractive. Ever wonder what other cultures find beautiful?

TEENY-TINY FEET

For nearly 1,000 years, Chinese men liked women to have dainty feet—so dainty that they could barely walk on them. This made the women virtually helpless and dependent on men to carry them from place to place, which was regarded as a sign of leisure and wealth. How did they get their feet so small? With the practice of foot binding, a technique invented in the 10th century. Here's how it worked: A toddler girl was taken to the local foot binder (yes, that was an occupation!), who bent her toes over and wrapped her feet so tightly with cloth that they couldn't grow. Foot binding hurt, and as the girl grew older, her foot bones and muscles became so mutilated that walking was excruciatingly painful. It started out as a fad among rich families, but by the 17th century, nearly every woman, rich and poor, in northern China—an estimated two billion of them—had her feet bound. There are still a few elderly women living today with mangled "golden lotus" feet (so called because they resemble tight flower buds), but foot binding was officially outlawed in 1949.

LONG NECKS

The Kayan-Padaung people of Thailand see long necks as a sign of beauty and wealth. That's not unusual, but the Kayan-Padaung take it several steps further: Beginning as early as age five, little girls have brass rings wrapped around their necks. As they get older, more and more rings—sometimes as many as 40—are added until their collarbones are compressed and their necks are stretched to a length of nearly 18 inches. In some villages, if a woman is found with another man, her husband may insist she remove her rings as punishment. This could have serious consequences: Without the rings to support it, the woman's stretched-out neck may be weak and misshapen. Neck-ringing is still practiced in some areas of Thailand, where the local people are known as (can you guess?) the Long Necks.

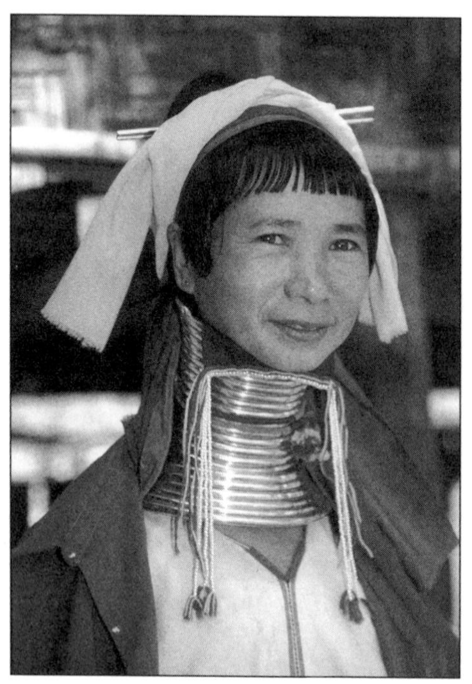

STUBBY TEETH

Wondering what to do in July and August? Why not

have your teeth filed down? On the Indonesian island of Bali, filing down the front teeth to flatten the edges and make them smaller is a practice that, according to legend, helps young Balinese men and women get rid of the forces of evil—lust, greed, anger, jealousy—lurking inside them. This rite of passage from youth into adulthood takes place in the summer months, usually between 4:00 and 6:00 a.m. During the ceremony, a Hindu priest uses a file, a small hammer, and a carver to grind down the sharp edges of the young person's teeth. It may sound like your worst dentist nightmare, but the Balinese have been doing it for more than 2,000 years.

PLATED LIPS

Imagine you are a young girl from the Suri people of Ethiopia, and you are planning to get married. Here's one way you'll get ready for your wedding: About six weeks before the happy day, your lower lip is pierced and a wooden plug is inserted into the hole. As the wound heals, bigger and bigger plugs are inserted into your lip until, eventually, you can fit an 8-inch disk made of wood or clay—one that you decorated yourself—into the hole. Now you're considered a truly beautiful bride. But try to imagine eating or talking with that giant plate in your lower lip. Many Suri women have their lower front teeth pulled to make the plate more comfortable, but some women just settle for a liquid diet. Lip plating is popular in several parts of Africa and in South America's Amazon region.

In cheerleader lingo, underpants are called *spankies*.

BIRD'S-EYE VIEW

Author Isabella Bird never did anything easy. In her quest to see the world, she always chose the road less traveled.

BABY BIRD

Born in 1831, Isabella Bird was small for her age and sickly for almost all of her childhood in Yorkshire, England. When she was 20, her family doctor suggested that travel might do her good. So Isabella's father gave her 100 pounds ($6,000 today) and told her to go wherever she liked. (Thanks, Dad!) She visited the United States for a few months, came home, and promptly published a book about her experiences, *The Englishwoman in America*. But the once-sickly girl had been bitten by the travel bug, so she set off to see more of the world.

MAUI WOW!

Bird credits her trip to Hawaii in 1872 with transforming her from a tourist into an adventurer. During her six months in that island paradise, she climbed to the top of Hawaii's volcanoes and trekked into remote valleys that most Hawaiians had never seen or even heard of. Afterward, she wrote another book about her trip—a pattern that would turn her into a professional writer and support her for the rest of her life.

ROCKY MOUNTAIN HIGH

Bird's next adventure was crossing the North American West in 1873 from Lake Tahoe to Colorado on horseback…alone. On the trek, her eyelids once froze shut in a snowstorm, and she ended up spending the winter in a cabin with an outlaw named Jim Nugent, who stole her heart. When he asked her to marry him, she said no. She later explained to a friend, "He is a man any woman might love but no sane woman would marry." (She was right—Nugent was killed in a gunfight soon after.)

WEST MEETS EAST

After a quick trip home to England, Bird decided that Asia would be next. So she journeyed to Japan and became one of the first Westerners to live among the Ainu, the aboriginal people of the island of Hokkaido, before traveling on to China and Southeast Asia. When she returned to England in 1880 to see her dying sister, she met and married her sister's Scottish doctor. That put the brakes on her traveling. But when her husband died five years later, she set out again—this time to Kashmir and Tibet. In India, she used some of the money she'd earned from the publication of her books to establish two hospitals in memory of her sister and husband. From India she crossed the Persian desert on a camel in the middle of winter, arriving in Tehran almost dead from hypothermia.

EVER ONWARD

Nearly every step of the way, Isabella turned her adventures into books. And they were so widely read that she became one of the most famous travelers of her era and was the first woman to be made a member of the Royal Geographic Society. At 66 she took her final journey, a trip up the Yangtze River in China…and was almost lynched by a mob who thought she was a witch. But she made it home safely once again. At age 72, while back home in Scotland getting ready for yet another trip, Bird fell ill and died. But her 16 books live on, and they have entertained readers ever since.

ISABELLA BIRD'S TRAVEL BOOKS: A SELECTED LIST

- *The Englishwoman in America* (1856)
- *The Hawaiian Archipelago* (1875)
- *A Lady's Life in the Rocky Mountains* (1879)
- *Unbeaten Tracks in Japan* (1880)
- *Journeys in Persia and Kurdistan* (1891)
- *Among the Tibetans* (1894)
- *The Yangtze Valley and Beyond* (1899)
- *Chinese Pictures* (1900)

UNEASY RIDERS

In the music world, a "contract rider" is a list of food and creature comforts that the pop star insists on having backstage before and after a concert. Some of them get pretty demanding!

STAR: Justin Bieber
DEMAND: Vitamin Water and Swedish Fish or Big Foots candy, plus T-shirts and socks of all sizes...except medium.

STAR: Gnarls Barkley
DEMAND: A bucket of Kentucky Fried Chicken, a dozen doughnuts (Dunkin' Donuts or Krispy Kreme), and a 2-pack of men's white athletic socks.

STAR: Taylor Swift
DEMAND: Twizzlers red licorice on Thursdays, dill pickles on Fridays, Ragú spaghetti on Saturday. Also Smart Water, Starbucks lattes, pumpkin loaf, macaroni and cheese, nacho fixings, fresh fruits and veggies, and... Ben and Jerry's ice cream daily.

STAR: Rihanna
DEMAND: A six-foot white cloth couch that is wide enough for her to take a nap on. Cheetah- or leopard-print throw pillows with no sequins, an animal-print throw rug, and Archipelago Black Forest Candles.

In Japan, McDonald's serves an "Ebisu" burger made of fish and shrimp.

STAR: John Mayer

DEMAND: Four soft-head toothbrushes, a bottle of Listerine, two small tubes of mint-flavored toothpaste (Sensodyne or Tom's of Maine), two packages of Altoids breath mints, four organic lip balms, some Gold Bond powder, and two tubes of Original Krazy Glue.

STAR: Red Hot Chili Peppers

DEMAND: Lucky Charms; whole, pitted dates; unsalted raw cashews; and plain rice cakes.

STAR: Christina Aguilera

DEMAND: A police escort from the airport to the stadium and "under no circumstances are the vehicles to be allowed to encounter any delays due to traffic." Also, Flintstones chewable vitamins, Oreos, and a bottle of chocolate Nesquik in her dressing room.

STAR: Jay-Z

DEMAND: Sugar-free Red Bull, hand sanitizer, fresh fruit, organic bread, a bottle of honey, orange juice (without pulp), and a bowl of Sour Patch Kids. He also requires a nice set of china dishes, cloth dinner napkins, and real silverware. And four golf carts.

STAR: Mariah Carey

DEMAND: Champagne, sugarless gum, tea service for eight, and a box of bendy straws.

King George VI of England's first name was actually Albert.

JANE GOODALL: CHIMP CHUM

"African wildlife adventurer" was hardly an occupation fit for a young lady in the 1930s. But Jane Goodall's mother told her, "You can do whatever you set your mind to." So she did.

DREAMS OF AFRICA

Valerie Jane Morris-Goodall was born curious. When she was a year and half old, she took a handful of earthworms to bed with her. Her mother found them and told Jane that they'd die without dirt, so the two of them returned the worms to their home in the garden. By the time Jane was five, she liked to hide for hours in the henhouse, waiting to see how a hen laid an egg, oblivious to the fact that her family was frantically searching for her. At age seven, she read *The Story of Dr. Dolittle* and *Tarzan of the Apes* and vowed to one day visit Africa to observe and write about animals. She made up stories about the animals that lived in her family's garden and even opened her own "conservatory" that included flowers, shells, and a human skeleton. When she turned 12, Goodall formed a nature club called the Alligator Society with her sister and some friends, and even published a small magazine filled with nature notes, drawings of insect anatomy, and their observations of animal behavior.

Vincent, the dog on *Lost*, was played by a female dog named Madison.

FIRST STOP, KENYA

In 1957 Goodall was 22 and working for a film studio in London when she received an invitation that would change her life. Family friends asked if she wanted to visit their farm in Kenya, Africa, and she jumped at the chance. After arriving in Kenya, she found she loved it so much that she immediately sought work so she could stay in that amazing country. As luck would have it, Louis Leakey, a famous paleontologist (a scientist who studies prehistoric life), needed a secretary and assistant. Goodall was hired to accompany Leakey and his wife Mary to East Africa's Olduvai Gorge to search for evidence of early humans. (A few years after that journey, the Leakeys found the remains of *Homo habilis*, the earliest human ancestor known to make and use tools.) Leakey was so impressed by Goodall's knowledge of animals, and her reliability, that he gave her another job—one that would become her life's work.

NEXT STOP, GOMBE

A group of chimpanzees were living near a lake in Tanganyika (what is now Tanzania), and Leakey asked Goodall to study them to see if they offered any insight into human ancestors. Leakey got funding from the National Geographic Society for the chimp study, but there was one important condition: Goodall was not allowed to travel the backcountry alone. There had been fighting among local rebels, and it was considered unsafe for a young woman to travel by herself. Goodall agreed to

Studies have found that men change their minds 2–3 times more often than women do.

the condition and invited her mother, Vanne, to join her. Off they went to Tanganyika.

JANE SEE, MONKEY DO

In July 1960, Goodall and her mother arrived at the Gombe Stream Game Reserve in western Tanganyika. They lived in a four-pole tent with a straw roof in the middle of a jungle teeming with leopards, cobras, and Cape buffalo. But the chimpanzees, which were known to live nearby, were very shy and hard to find. Every morning at 5:30, Goodall left her tent, armed with binoculars and a pad and pencil, in search of them. She wandered the jungle for weeks before she finally found the key—a spot high on a mountain where she could sit and observe the chimps in the valley below. Soon Goodall was able to tell the animals apart and, instead of numbering them scientifically, she gave them names like David Greybeard, Goliath, William, and Flo.

BIG DISCOVERIES

Within two weeks, Goodall had observed behaviors that had never been reported before. Chimps had always been thought to be vegetarians, but she witnessed David Greybeard eat a pig, and saw chimpanzees hunt other animals, including monkeys and other small mammals. Even more remarkable, she saw the chimps using primitive tools—blades of grass to dig termites out of their nests, and leaves to collect water. This changed the world of anthropology—until then, it was believed that humans were the only mammals that used tools. When she told Louis Leakey of her discovery, he wrote, "Now we must redefine 'tool,' redefine 'man,' or accept chimpanzees as humans."

WELCOME, GRUB

Even with her busy research schedule, Goodall managed to have a personal life, too. In 1964 she married Baron Hugo van Lawick, a Dutch photographer sent by *National Geographic* to film the chimpanzees. A year later, when a television documentary about her aired, the 30-year-old Goodall became internationally famous. In 1967 she gave birth to her son, Hugo Eric Louis van Lawick. It was a big name for a little boy, so they simply called him "Grub." Goodall raised Grub "in the chimp way," never leaving him alone for the first three years of his life while he stayed with her in Tanganyika. Grub's first sentence was, "That big lion out there eat me."

THE GOOD, THE BAD, AND THE UGLY

Over the next 30 years, Goodall and her teams of assistants found countless similarities between chimpanzee and human development. They witnessed chimps using nonverbal behaviors to show their emotions, like patting each other on the back, holding hands, tickling each other, and holding grudges if they were offended. They even saw a teenage chimp named Spindle "adopt" a three-year-old orphan named Mel.

But as warm and loving as the families could be, Goodall also began to discover a darker—and truly shocking—side to the chimps' behavior. In one case, a mother and daughter stole, killed, and ate the babies of their friends. At other times, bands of rival chimpanzees ganged up on their neighbors and tried to kill them. Worst of all, in 1974 a four-year chimp war began at Gombe, ending only when one group had completely killed off the other. This was the first record of long-term warfare in nonhuman primates.

GOODALL NOW

Jane Goodall's work in the jungle, far from civilization, didn't shield her from life's sometimes painful realities. After divorcing her first husband, she married Derek Bryceson, director of national parks in Tanzania, in 1975 and the two pursued their shared passion—protecting the African wilderness. That same year, four Gombe staff members were kidnapped and held for ransom. They were eventually released, but by then, her new husband was locked in a battle with cancer, which he lost in 1980. After so many years of field research, Dame Jane Goodall (she was awarded the title at Buckingham Palace in 2004) now travels the world as a lecturer and official United Nations Messenger of Peace.

When Jane Goodall was 1½ years old, her father gave her a toy chimpanzee that she named Jubilee, after a chimp at the London zoo. It is her most treasured possession and sits on her dresser today.

Herbert Lapidus invented Odor Eater insoles in the 1970s to cure his wife's stinky feet.

ONE WIFE + TWO HUSBANDS

Most people know that in some cultures, a man can have more than one wife. But did you know that in some societies, women have more than one husband?

THE MEN OF THE HOUSE

Polyandry is the official term for a woman marrying more than one man. In many cultures throughout history, there was a good reason for this: protection. When one husband had to leave his family for long periods to hunt for food, it was considered wise to have a second husband who could stay with the family and children.

Often the two husbands were brothers. In some societies, land was extremely scarce, so rather than divide up a small plot between two families, brothers would sometimes share the land, a wife, and kids. Polyandry was once common in Nepal, Tibet, Africa, and Polynesia, and it's still found today in isolated areas of Asia and Latin America. Unlike the most common type of *polygamy*, where a man usually gets to pick his wives, in polyandry, the women generally don't get to pick their husbands—they choose her.

> "People shop for a bathing suit with more care than they do a husband or wife. The rules are the same. Look for something you'll feel comfortable wearing. Allow for room to grow."
>
> —Erma Bombeck

WANTED: PRINCESS

When Britain's Prince Charles was almost 30, his family decided it was high time that the future king of England got himself a wife. Here's how they went about finding one for him.

JOB DESCRIPTION

In the late 1970s, Prince Charles of England was nearly 30 years old. He'd done a fair amount of dating, and he'd come to rely on the advice of his great uncle, "Uncle Dickie" Mountbatten, in matters of romance. Until then, Uncle Dickie had told the young prince to keep his options open and date many women. But as Charles neared 30 years old, Uncle Dickie said it was time to get down to the business of finding a wife—a future king just couldn't be single. He told Charles to choose a "suitable, attractive and sweet-charactered girl before she met someone else she might fall for." There were several strict requirements for the bride-to-be. She had to a) come from a noble—preferably British—family, b) be of child-bearing age, c) never have been divorced, d) not be Catholic, and e) have had no previous romantic involvements that might embarrass the royal family.

THE CANDIDATES

As the prince dated potential fiancées, the British people were kept guessing as to which woman might be their next queen. But none of the ladies had the perfect

In the 1100s, Empress Matilda of England escaped a band of kidnappers by traveling through...

résumé. Princess Marie Astrid of Luxembourg was a Catholic, Laura Jo Watkins was American, and Fiona Watson had been a *Penthouse* model (a huge no-no). For a time, a woman named Davina Sheffield was the leading candidate...until a previous boyfriend blabbed to the press that they had once lived together, unmarried. Camilla Shand, the one woman that the prince seemed to really care for, also had a "past" (a previous serious boyfriend), so she was out. At last, Lord Mountbatten suggested his 21-year-old granddaughter Amanda Knatchbull. But in 1979, just as Charles and Amanda were warming to each other, Uncle Dickie, his wife, and Amanda's brother were tragically killed by Irish Republican Army terrorists. Amanda decided it was dangerous to get too close to the royal family, so when Prince Charles proposed to her, she turned him down.

NEXT APPLICANT, PLEASE

Charles was now 31 years old, and the clock was ticking—the pressure for him to find a wife became enormous. Enter Lady Diana Spencer. The 19-year-old kindergarten aide was the younger sister of a woman Charles had previously dated, and she had blossomed into a beautiful young lady. But her résumé wasn't impressive, either: Diana had flunked out of her O-levels (the British equivalent of high school) twice, so going to college wasn't an option for her. Instead, she'd held a few jobs as a housekeeper, nanny, and teacher's aide. But romantically she was a blank slate—she'd had no serious boyfriends, leading the British newspapers to describe her as "a woman with no past." That made her exactly what Uncle Dickie had recommended for Charles. The prince dated Diana through the summer and fall of 1980 and found her reserved, sweet, and pleasant enough. But his father, Prince Philip, pressured him to pop the question soon because, as Philip put it, "any delay would risk Diana's reputation." The dutiful son proposed, Diana accepted, and they were engaged. By that time, England and the world had fallen in love with "Shy Di," as the press nicknamed her.

YOU'RE HIRED!

After "the wedding of the century" in London in July 1981—a ceremony that was attended by 3,500 guests and watched by 750 million TV viewers—Diana lived the life of a modern princess under constant scrutiny by the press and public. She eventually had two sons and became a powerful advocate for sufferers of AIDS and leprosy. Even though the tabloid news paparazzi harassed her around the clock, she managed to raise her boys, found a hospital, and form an organization that won the Nobel Peace Prize for its work to ban land mines. Her marriage, however, was a disaster.

Krusty the Clown on *The Simpsons* was inspired by a real TV kids' show host, Rusty Nails.

TAKE THIS JOB AND SHOVE IT

Early on, Diana discovered that being a princess wasn't a fairy-tale life. Her marriage to Charles, she later said, was more of a business arrangement than a romantic one, and despite being surrounded by press, adoring fans, and royal servants, Diana led a lonely existence. Camilla Shand, now a married woman, had reappeared in Charles's life and, as Princess Diana said in a TV interview, "There were three of us in the marriage." Charles and Diana divorced in 1996.

Sadly, only a year later, Diana and her new boyfriend, Dodi Fayed, were killed in a high-speed car crash in Paris. Why were they speeding? They were trying to escape the photographers who dogged their every move. There would be no fairy-tale ending for Diana. Thousands of people lined the streets of London to watch her casket pass by on its way to her funeral, which 2.5 billion people watched on TV—a global outpouring of grief for the shy girl who had become the most beloved princess of modern times.

NEXT GENERATION

Prince Charles eventually married Camilla Shand, by then a divorcée (so much for Rule C) and known as Camilla Parker Bowles. And in 2010, Charles and Diana's elder son, 28-year-old Prince William, became engaged to a new "perfect choice for princess," Kate Middleton. And the story continues.

Japan once had an amusement park based on the book *Anne of Green Gables*.

THE BEST PRINCESS MOVIES EVER

Because everybody needs a little fantasy now and then.

THE PRINCESS BRIDE (1987)

"Gather round, kids of all ages, as swashbuckling Westley (Cary Elwes) sets out to rescue the impossibly beautiful Buttercup (Robin Wright) from a monarchy full of dastardly types. As you watch this enchanting fantasy, feel free to be thrilled or to giggle, 'as you wish.'"

—***Time*** **magazine**

EVER AFTER (1998)

"Exquisite retelling of the Cinderella story with a luminous Drew Barrymore as the young charmer who rises above her station to steal the heart of the prince (Dougray Scott). A live-action fairy tale filled with heart and humor, and just the right amount of magic."

—***DVD and Video Guide***

THE PRINCESS DIARIES (2001)

"This Cinderella fantasy transforms a geek (Anne Hathaway) into a princess, and teaches a few life lessons along the way. Julie Andrews is delightful as the imperious Clarisse. Hathaway and Heather Matarazzo are a refreshing change of pace: They actually look like ordinary high-school students."

—***TV Guide's Movie Guide***

STARDUST (2007)

"This irresistible fantasy about a young man (Charlie Cox) who enters a magical realm to find a falling star (Claire Danes) is exciting, funny, adventurous, magical, and very romantic. The special effects are great, but the characters are even better."

—***New York Daily News***

ENCHANTED (2005)

"Classic Disney animation meets contemporary urban chaos in this romantic comedy. A frightened princess (Amy Adams) is banished from her magical animated homeland to modern-day New York City, where she soon finds herself falling for a friendly but flawed divorce lawyer (Patrick Dempsey)."

—***AllMovie DVD Guide***

Highest-paid animal actors: Bears make about $20,000 per day. (Dogs and cats: about $300.)

THE PAGE OF BOOBS

Since this is a book about girls, we figured it needed at least one page about boobs.

• A woman's breasts are rarely the same size. The left one is usually bigger.

• The word "bra" is short for "brassiere," which comes from the French *braciere*—a shield worn by soldiers.

• At Hong Kong's Polytechnic University, you can get a degree in Bra Studies.

• One test that actresses and models use to see if their breasts are sagging: Put a pencil under one breast, and if you can hold it there, your breasts are sagging. Bette Midler once said, "A pencil? I could put a typewriter under there and it wouldn't fall out."

• An average adult breast weighs one pound.

• A woman's breasts account for about 2 percent of her body weight.

• In Dutch, the word for bra is *bustehouder*.

• Actual casting notice for one of the *Pirates of the Caribbean* movies: "Wanted: Fit female models. Must have a lean dancer body. Must have real breasts. Do not apply if you have implants."

• Victoria's Secret sells a bra that's inset with 1,300 gemstones, including diamonds and rubies. They'll even throw in the matching panties! Cost: $15 million.

Traditional Christmas Eve dinner in Armenia: fried fish, lettuce, and spinach.

i spy

Not all spies drive fast cars and play with guns. Sometimes they're the people you'd least suspect...like a chef, or a glamorous movie star.

CHILD'S PLAY

Before Julia Child became a famous chef, she was a spy for the U.S. Office of Strategic Services. The OSS (which later became the CIA) was formed by President Franklin D. Roosevelt during World War II. Besides helping to get the scoop on enemy activities, Child cooked up a way to keep sharks from accidentally detonating underwater mines: a paste with a "special shark-repelling ingredient" that was smeared over the mines. The special ingredient? Rotten shark meat.

STAR POWER

If you like your cell phone, thank Hedy Lamarr, an Austrian-born actress who was a Hollywood star in the 1930s and '40s. In 1942 Lamarr, who had always excelled at math and science, partnered with musician George Antheil to invent a "secret communication system" that could remotely guide torpedoes by using radio signals. The idea was ahead of its time: The military couldn't figure out how to make it work until 1962, when navy engineers adapted the system to guide nuclear missiles. Years later, civilian engineers adapted it again to telephone communications...and created the cell phones we use today.

Human speech involves at least 100 muscles in the face and throat.

AMAZING GRACE

Grace Murray Hopper was a small woman with a great head for numbers...and she used those numbers to change our world.

MS. CURIOUS

Grace Murray (1906–92) wasn't your average kid. When she was seven, her mother came home to find seven alarm clocks in pieces on the kitchen table. Grace wanted to know what made a clock tick, so she'd taken one apart. When she couldn't put it back together, she tried another. And another. And another. It was a glimpse of the remarkable qualities—patience, persistence, and perseverance—that would eventually make her the godmother of the computer.

NO IS NOT IN HER VOCABULARY

It didn't hurt that Grace was also a whiz with numbers. In 1934 she became the first woman to earn a Ph.D in math from Yale University, married a professor named Vincent Hopper, and started teaching at Vassar College. When World War II broke out in 1941, she decided to offer her math skills to the military and tried to join the U.S. Navy...but they turned her down. Why? At 34, she was considered too old, and with just 105 pounds on her 5'6" frame, she was 16 pounds underweight, according to navy standards. But Hopper wouldn't take no for an answer. She petitioned the navy for the next two years

Girls are more likely than boys to use a computer for school assignments.

until finally, in 1943, they let her into the Naval Reserve. She was assigned to the Naval Bureau of Ordnance's Computation Project at Harvard University, a pioneering computer lab—and that's where she met Howard Aiken and the Mark I.

MAKING HER MARK

Aiken was the Harvard genius behind the first modern supercomputer. Brilliant and eccentric, he sized up colleagues quickly, and if they weren't up to snuff, he told them so. Grace Hopper recalled years later that when she reported to Aiken's lab to start work, he gave her a quick look and barked, "Where have you been?" Then he assigned her to program his team's new computer, a 55-foot long, 8-foot wide, 5-ton tangle of relays, switches, and vacuum tubes called the Mark I. For Hopper, it was love at first sight—love for the computer, that is. She quickly became a top Mark I programmer and wrote the manual on how to program it. Later, she partnered with Aiken and his team on the development of the Mark II and Mark III.

GOING BUGGY

Engineers as far back as 1874 had used the term "bug" to describe a glitch in a design or mechanism. But it was Grace Hopper who made the term synonymous with computers. While checking out a bad switch on the Mark II in 1947, she found the source of the problem: a dead moth. She taped the moth into the repair log with a note that read: “First actual case of a bug being found” and told her colleagues that the computer had been “debugged.” The term has been associated with her ever since. Today, the page from the logbook—with the moth still taped to it—is on display in the Naval Surface Warfare Center Computer Museum in Dahlgren, Virginia.

GRANDMA COBOL

But Grace Hopper’s greatest contribution may be how she helped make computers a tool that everyone could use. Early computers could only be programmed using complex mathematical language that no one but highly trained mathematicians and engineers knew. And most computer experts assumed it would always be that way. Grace Hopper saw it differently. She wondered, “What if computers could be programmed using word-based commands that anyone could learn?” Then, she reasoned, computers could be used for business, entertainment, games—almost any application that could be imagined. In 1955, after many small steps along the way, Grace produced a program called Flow-Matic, which became the basis for the computer language COBOL (Common Business Oriented Language), which is still used today. Computer historians now call her the “Grandmother of COBOL.”

NAVY BLUE

All the while that Grace Hopper was computing, she

First band to stream a live concert on YouTube: U2, in October 2009.

continued to serve in the navy, rising through the ranks of the Naval Reserve to become a commander. The navy and computers were her life: Divorced in 1945, she never remarried or had children. By 1966 she had served beyond the 20 years allowed for reservists and was told that she had to retire. So, reluctantly, she did. But by then, the navy had decided to convert all of its weapons and missile systems programs to COBOL, and they quickly realized that no one knew COBOL better than Grace Hopper. So they begged her to come back. She served for another 20 years and finally retired as a rear admiral, one of the first women ever to achieve that rank. At 79, she was the oldest active-duty military officer in U.S. history.

It was only fitting that her retirement ceremony was held aboard the legendary warship USS *Constitution*, the oldest active ship in the navy. She was the first winner of the National Medal of Technology (1991) and even the first computer science "Man of the Year" (1969). Grace Hopper died in 1992 at the age of 85.

GRACE HOPPER QUOTES

- "Humans are allergic to change. They love to say, 'We've always done it this way.' I try to fight that. That's why I have a clock on my wall that runs counterclockwise."
- "If it's a good idea, go ahead and do it. It's much easier to apologize than it is to get permission."

GIRL GEEKS

Think all internet geniuses are over 30? Think again. These teenage girls started their own internet companies—and they're kicking some serious cyber-butt.

GIRL GEEK: Melissa Sconyers
HER STARTUP: Ativity.com
HER STORY: By the time Melissa was six months old, she was already playing with a computer keyboard. She was creating Web pages by the age of 10, and at 16 the Houston, Texas, teen started her own web business: Ativity.com, a web-design studio. Soon she was charging clients $1,000 per page and earning tens of thousands of dollars a year. That was in 1994. Sconyers has gone on to become an internationally recognized expert in online marketing and advertising.

GIRL GEEK: Catherine Cook
HER STARTUP: myYearbook.com
HER STORY: In 2005, when Catherine was a 15-year-old sophomore at Montgomery High School in New Jersey, she and her brother Dave, 17, decided to turn their high-school yearbook into a social networking site. Their website took off, attracting not only other teens but also big advertisers like Neutrogena and Disney, and by 2006 they had three million members. Some investors offered to buy them out for a few thousand dollars, but they said, "No way." Good decision—by 2009

the site had more than 20 million members all over the world and was making Catherine and her brother $20 million a year.

GIRL GEEK: Ashley Qualls
HER STARTUP: WhateverLife.com
HER STORY: All that 14-year-old Ashley wanted was a place online to post her portfolio of fashion designs and art. It was 2004, and the Lincoln Park, Michigan, native didn't like what was available—so she decided to make her own site. WhateverLife.com soon became *the* spot for teen girls to learn how to create their own websites and graphic designs. Ashley provided all the tools they needed for free on WhateverLife.com. She worked out of her basement (she still does), but soon had her mom and friends working for her (they still do, only now

they do it full-time). According to Google, Ashley's site gets 60 million page views a month. That's more than the circulations of *Seventeen*, *Teen Vogue*, and *CosmoGirl* combined. When Ashley was 17, someone offered to buy WhateverLife.com for $1.5 million and the car of her choice, but Ashley declined. Why? "I don't even have my license yet."

GIRL GEEK: Jessica Mah
HER STARTUP: InDinero.com
HER STORY: New York native Jessica began programming PCs at age nine. She started her first internet business at 12, and by age 15, she was already in college. That was where she created a website called intershipIN.com, a hugely successful site that paired college students with internships. At 19 she was able to get major Silicon Valley investors to contribute $1 million in seed money to back her latest startup—InDinero.com, a sleek, simple website with tools that help small businesses track their finances. Called "the closest thing we've got to a female Mark Zuckerberg" (the billionaire founder of Facebook), Jessica is a rising star among the ranks of young internet entrepreneurs. Says one of her biggest fans, famed programmer Paul Graham, "She's going to win at whatever game she plays."

THE LADIES' ROOM

Even glamorous women have to go to the bathroom. Check out these star-studded bathroom facts.

• Madonna's touring contract specifies that all toilet seats backstage and in her dressing room have to be brand new and still in their plastic wrappers. And when she leaves, the toilet seats must be destroyed so they can't be sold as Madonna souvenirs on eBay.

• Actress Catherine Zeta-Jones says, "For a marriage to be a success, the woman and man should have her and his own bathroom. The end."

• After the 1979 Academy Awards, Meryl Streep misplaced the Oscar that she'd won for *Kramer vs. Kramer*. Where did she leave it? On the back of a toilet in the ladies' room.

• Musician Alicia Keys says, "If I want to be alone—someplace I can write, I can read, I can pray, I can cry, I can do whatever I want—I go to the bathroom."

• Where does British actress and screenwriter Emma Thompson like to write? In one of the bathrooms in her Scottish estate. That's where she wrote her Oscar-winning screenplay for *Sense and Sensibility*. She keeps the Oscar statuette on a shelf in that same bathroom—right next to the one she won for Best Actress in *Howard's End*.

The length of your arms, stretched out, is about equal to your height.

GUDRIDUR THE GREAT

Have you ever felt like doing something, but were afraid to because no one had ever done it before? As this explorer proved, it's okay to be the first to do something…in fact, it's great.

BRAVE NEW WORLD

When a Viking girl named Gudridur Eiríksdóttir was born in the late 10th century, her home island of Iceland was like the Wild West of Europe—untamed and full of adventurous people. As a teenager, she set off with her family across the storm-tossed North Atlantic to settle in Greenland—but the dangerous voyage killed everyone except her. She made a life for herself in Greenland and got married, but her husband soon died in a plague epidemic. Gudridur married again, and she and her new husband led an expedition to Vinland (now Newfoundland, Canada) in 1004. There she gave birth

to a son, Snorri—the first child of European descent to be born in the Americas.

ALWAYS A TRAVELER

During the next three years, Gudridur and her family explored their new home of North America, venturing as far south as what is now the island of Manhattan. But they occasionally had trouble with native tribes, and in one skirmish, Gudridur's husband, Thorfinnur, was killed. Widowed again, Gudridur returned home to Iceland and became a nun. Some thought that would put an end to her wanderings, but Gudridur's travels weren't over yet. A convert to Christianity, she decided to pay the pope a visit—in Rome—to give him a report on Christianity in Iceland and tell him of her explorations of the New World.

THE LONG WALK

Getting to Rome from Iceland was an adventure all its own. At a time when women didn't travel alone, Gudridur sailed by herself across 600 miles of open sea from Iceland to Denmark, and then walked an amazing 1,000 miles across Europe to Rome. And then, after she had her chat with the pope, she turned around and walked all the way back to Denmark, then sailed home. Since then, stories of Gudridur's voyages have made her a folk hero in her native Iceland. In 2000 Iceland's president dedicated a statue to her in her hometown of Laugarbrekka, declaring her "the greatest female explorer of all time."

...upside down on a calculator: hILLBILLIES (53177187714).

WHAT KIND OF ROCK STAR ARE YOU?

Take this quiz and find out!

1. You're attending a formal event, so you wear:

A. A sweet, flowing gown in muted tones, and a pair of strappy heels.

B. A skin-tight asymmetrical dress, as short as it can be, with a pair of stiletto heels, of course!

C. An old T-shirt that you cut up and transformed into a mini dress, a leather jacket, and your trusty beat-up Converse sneakers.

D. A latex jumpsuit with a wedding veil and a pair of five-inch platform shoes that light up. (You like to make an entrance.)

2. If you could have any pet, you would choose:

A. A horse. What could be better than a gallop on the beach at sunset?

B. A cat. You love how sassy and intuitive they are.

C. A dog—the bigger, the better. They truly are a girl's best friend.

D. A cheetah. Anything normal would be a bore.

3. Your favorite dessert is:

A. Apple pie—simple and classic.

How much does it cost to run a full-page color ad in *Vogue* magazine? About $90,000.

B. Strawberry ice cream. (You have a thing for the color pink.)

C. Chocolate pudding—perfect for flinging in a spontaneous food fight.

D. Green Jell-O. It's so awful, it's awesome!

4. It's movie night, so you want to watch:

A. A romance like *The Notebook*. You adore classic love stories.

B. A comedy like *Superbad*. You know it will make you laugh till you cry.

C. A thriller like *The Sixth Sense*. There's nothing better than being on the edge of your seat.

D. An "indie" film—the weirder, the better. You like movies that really make you think.

5. When you want to relax, you:

A. Chill at home with the ones you love and get back to your roots.

B. Go out with your best friends and party till dawn.

C. Go to a theme park and ride the biggest roller coaster—you love living life in the fast lane.

D. What do you mean, "relax"?

6. Your ideal vacation is:

A. A week at the beach filled with lots of sunbathing and moonlit walks.

B. A trip to Paris for *l'art* and *le shopping*.

C. Backpacking through Europe with no agenda other than whatever sounds good at the moment.

D. A trip to Tokyo to check out the amazing street fashion and immerse yourself in the culture.

7. You are often told:

A. "You are so sweet! You always have something nice to say."

B. "You are so fun! You always have something awesome planned for the evening."

C. "You are a wild child! There is never a dull moment with you."

D. "There is no one like you. You are a true original."

8. It's raining. Time to cuddle up and read:

A. *Pride and Prejudice*

B. *Eat, Pray, Love*

C. A *Harry Potter* book

D. *Interview with the Vampire*

IF YOU SCORED…

Mostly A's, you're a Country Rocker.

Like Taylor Swift, you are sweet and traditional. You believe in romance and aren't afraid to show it. You're willing to wait for your true love to sweep you off your feet. A down-to-earth girl, you'll always remember to be yourself, no matter where fame takes you.

Mostly B's, you're a Pop Rocker

Like Katy Perry, you have an infectious sense of fun. You can laugh at yourself, and you're the life of the party wherever you go. People are drawn to your magnetic personality and zest for life.

Mostly C's, you're a Punk Rocker

Like Avril Lavigne, you're shy, but when you cut loose, there's no holding you back. You're down with being one of the guys or chilling with the girls. You take every project very seriously. You are the essence of casual cool and never try to be something you're not.

Mostly D's, you're a Shock Rocker

Like Lady Gaga, you can be over-the-top intense, but people are hypnotized by your wild and unpredictable energy. You make a statement with everything you do and are always looking for ways to try new things and expand boundaries.

Only female bees sting.

KNOCK! KNOCK!

Who's really *there?*

Q: Knock! Knock!
A: Who's there?
Q: Figs.
A: Figs who?
Q: Figs the doorbell—it's broken.

Q: Knock! Knock!
A: Who's there?
Q: Cargo.
A: Cargo who?
Q: Cargo beep-beep!

Q: Knock! Knock!
A: Who's there?
Q: Norma Lee.
A: Norma Lee who?
Q: Norma Lee I have my key.

Q: Knock! Knock!
A: Who's there?
Q: Waddle.
A: Waddle who?
Q: Waddle you give me to go away?

Q: Knock! Knock!
A: Who's there?
Q: Anita.
A: Anita who?
Q: Anita tissue. Achoo!

Q: Knock! Knock!
A: Who's there?
Q: Dishes.
A: Dishes who?
Q: Dishes your friend. Open the door!

Q: Knock! Knock!
A: Who's there?
Q: Sara.
A: Sara who?
Q: Sara doctor in the house?

Q: Knock! Knock!
A: Who's there?
Q: Baby owl.
A: Baby owl who?
Q: Baby owl see you later, baby I won't.

Bloodhounds can follow a scent that's as much as four days old.

WITH THIS RING...

You know how some couples have their wedding rings inscribed with romantic sayings? It turns out, not all of the inscriptions are hearts and flowers. Here are some we found on wedding and bridal websites—some funny, some weird, and all real.

You are SO mine.

IT'S ABOUT TIME, DORK!

Worth the wait!

Happy now? Good.

If removed,
alarm will sound.

**Wonder Twin
powers, activate!**

*I love you more
than a fat kid
loves cake.*

*999,995 more
years to go.*

Puky loves Limpy.

Two wishes left.

*To infinity
and beyond.*

A perfect fit.

His:
Frankenstein
Hers:
Bride of Frankenstein

PUT ME BACK ON!

THE LADY WITH THE LAMP

Many people think that Florence Nightingale invented nursing. She didn't. But she worked tirelessly throughout her life to make nursing a respectable profession—and saved countless lives in the process. Here are 10 facts about the most famous nurse in history.

1. She was named after the city where she was born in 1820: Florence, Italy.

2. Nightingale came from a wealthy family that employed 70 gardeners on their estate in Derbyshire, England, as well as countless cooks, cleaners, and ladies' maids. Florence never had to lift a finger to help around the mansion. In fact, she didn't even dress herself or do her own hair until she was 33—until then, her personal maid did it all for her.

3. When Florence was 24, she received what she later said was a "spiritual calling" and decided to become a nurse. Her parents were shocked—at the time, most nurses were nuns or prostitutes, and getting a nursing job would ruin her reputation. But Florence begged her father to let her study medicine and work in a hospital. He said no. Seven years later, after she'd rejected several marriage proposals and had a nervous breakdown, he finally said yes.

4. In 1853, after attending a German training school for nurses, Nightingale became superintendent of the Institution for Sick Gentlewomen in Distressed Circumstances in London, where she learned how to organize and manage a hospital. A year later, the 34-year-old Nightingale took a team of nurses to Constantinople (now Istanbul), Turkey, to care for British soldiers wounded in the Crimean War. The hospital conditions there were horrifying: Men were crammed into filthy beds while still in their uniforms, which were encrusted with grime and blood. Simply by cleaning up the men and the hospital, Florence and her team saved countless lives by slowing the spread of infection and disease.

5. Nightingale earned the nickname "the Lady with the Lamp" when she was serving in Constantinople. There, she often worked through the night caring for the sick and dying, carrying an oil lamp from bed to bed.

6. Nightingale returned home in 1856. After all the horrors she'd seen in Constantinople, she suffered from a nervous condition that today would be diagnosed as PTSD—post-traumatic stress disorder, a condition she would battle for the rest of her life.

7. Despite her fragile mental state, Nightingale continued working in England. She overhauled the British hospital system, and then laid the foundation for professional nursing by opening her own school at St. Thomas' Hospital in London. And, understanding that tainted water could cause cholera and other diseases, she helped the British government in India redesign their waste-removal and water-supply systems.

8. Florence Nightingale became the foremost expert of the 1800s on nursing and hospital organization. In 1859 she published a guidebook, *Notes on Nursing*, which became a multimillion best-seller.

9. Though often bedridden herself, Nightingale introduced many innovative ideas for patient care, such as bells that patients could ring to call for a nurse, dumbwaiters (small elevators) to bring food to the hospital rooms, and hot water piped to all the floors.

10. During the American Civil War, the U.S. Army contacted Nightingale in England and asked her to become a consultant to help the Union prepare its medical crews and hospitals.

Youngest Associated Press Athlete of the Year: 15-year-old golfer Marlene Bauer, in 1949.

BARBIE FACTS

The very first Barbie doll appeared on the scene in 1959 wearing a black-and-white-striped bathing suit and her signature ponytail. Cost: $3.00. Here are more facts about America's favorite classic doll.

• Where did Barbie and her boyfriend Ken get their names? Ruth Handler, Barbie's inventor, named them after her son and daughter.

• Barbie has had more than 43 pets, including 21 dogs, 12 horses, 3 ponies, 6 cats, a parrot, a chimpanzee, a panda, a lion cub, a giraffe, and a zebra.

• In 2004 Mattel announced that Barbie had broken up with Ken and was dating a cool boogie-boarding doll named Blaine, from Australia. (Barbie and Ken got back together in 2006.)

• In 2000 Barbie finally got a belly button.

• According to Barbie's official bio, her full name is Barbara Millicent Roberts, and she's from Willows, Wisconsin.

• Negative Message Barbie: A 1965 version of the doll came with a booklet called *How to Lose Weight*. On the back of the book was Barbie's secret: "Don't eat."

• Barbie's first job: fashion model. Since then, she's had more than 80 careers, including paleontologist and presidential candidate.

• In 2009 Totally Tattoos Barbie was released with stick-on tattoos, including one for her lower back.

According to polls, 46% of teenage girls use sunscreen regularly; only 30% of teen boys do.

I'M AYLAH FROM KANSAS

Our next "real girl" interview is with a 12-year-old from Kansas. She's an environmentalist Gemini, and she sees the world a little differently than most kids—because she's deaf. Here's her story.

- **My odd name:** My parents named me Aylah after the strong-willed female character from the 1980s book *The Clan of the Cave Bear*. Little did they know just how strong-willed I could be!
- **My home:** I live in two places. From Monday through Thursday I live in the dorms at the Kansas School for the Deaf. The rest of the time I live at home with my parents, sisters Zeva and Ashley, little brother Bodhi, and my gray tiger-striped cat, Puck.
- **Communication:** My friends and I use American Sign Language (ASL) to communicate. My family is also fluent in ASL, so there's no problem "talking" with them.
- **Hobbies:** Being on the computer and playing with artsy graphics is what I love most. But I also love to read! *The Sisters Grimm*, *Uglies*, and *Twilight* are on my bookshelf right now.
- **Sports:** I'll do just about any sport, but my favorites are volleyball, basketball, and track & field.
- **My BFF's:** Ranata and Tiffany, who live at the dorm with me. We love to practice synchronized cheers, have sporty competitions, and sometimes we'll dress up—like in biker clothes and pretend to be bad! When we're not together, we video-chat on our computers.
- **Favorite hangout:** The mall.
- **Secret indulgence:** I love to eat! Italian is my favorite. My

friends say I could be a food critic because I have a very sensitive palate.

- **School dances:** My school holds dances, but unlike schools for hearing kids, we don't have music. We dress up, hang with friends, and show off our latest synchronized cheers.
- **Game night with the fam:** I love to play *Apples to Apples* or watch a good movie with my family. Mom's homemade popcorn is the best!
- **Surprising fact:** Though I can't hear music at all, I love to dance and sing.
- **My dream:** To go to MIT and become an environmental engineer. I want to create ways to make "going green" easy on everyone and on the planet. I also want to travel around the world to study various forms of sign language.
- **My heroes:** Helen Keller (activist, author) and Marlee Matlin (actress)—two deaf women who went on to do amazing things in their lives.
- **My motto:** "Never give up."

* * *

NO-POO

Some hair experts say that frequent use of shampoo causes hair to become oily. Researchers have found that the more oil (sebum) you strip from your hair, the more oil your head will produce. There's even a "No-Poo" movement, which suggests ditching the shampoo completely and washing your hair with baking soda, followed by a rinse of apple cider vinegar, once a week. They say it makes your hair shinier, silkier, and healthier. If you can't bring yourself to go completely without shampoo, try gradually increasing the number of days between shampooing.

...A: Tapputi, a Mesopotamian woman who made perfume around 2000 B.C.

MAGICAL 9

Is math your favorite subject? Whether it is or not, you'll be amazed by these sequences based on the number 9. We're not sure why they work, but you may want to get a calculator and try them yourself!

ANY NUMBER GETS YOU NINE

Try this little trick. Take any two-digit number (37, for example), add the digits (3+7=10), then subtract that amount from your original number (37 – 10 = 27). The result will be always be a multiple of 9 (27 = 3 x 9). And if you add the two digits in that result, they will always add up to 9: (2 + 7 = 9)!

Here are some more amazing quirks based on the number 9.

NINES AND ONES

0 x 9 + 1 = 1
1 x 9 + 2 = 11
12 x 9 + 3 = 111
123 x 9 + 4 = 1,111
1,234 x 9 + 5 = 11,111
12,345 x 9 + 6 = 111,111
123,456 x 9 + 7 = 1,111,111
1,234,567 x 9 + 8 = 11,111,111
12,345,678 x 9 + 9 = 111,111,111
123,456,789 x 9 + 10 = 1,111,111,111

Author J. M. Barrie donated all the proceeds from his book *Peter Pan* to a children's hospital.

GOING UP, GOING DOWN

1 x 8 + 1 = 9

12 x 8 + 2 = 98

123 x 8 + 3 = 987

1,234 x 8 + 4 = 9,876

12,345 x 8 + 5 = 98,765

123,456 x 8 + 6 = 987,654

1,234,567 x 8 + 7 = 9,876,543

12,345,678 x 8 + 8 = 98,765,432

123,456,789 x 8 + 9 = 987,654,321

IT'S ALL NINE TO ME

Multiply 9 by any number from 1 to 10, and the digits in your product will always add up to 9!

1 x 9 = 9	(0 + 9) = 9
2 x 9 = 18	(1 + 8) = 9
3 x 9 = 27	(2 + 7) = 9
4 x 9 = 36	(3 + 6) = 9
5 x 9 = 45	(4 + 5) = 9
6 x 9 = 54	(5 + 4) = 9
7 x 9 = 63	(6 + 3) = 9
8 x 9 = 72	(7 + 2) = 9
9 x 9 = 81	(8 + 1) = 9
10 x 9 = 90	(9 + 0) = 9

More math magic: 1x9+1+9=19; 2x9+2+9=29. This formula works up to 9x9+9+9=99.

TURNABOUT IS FAIR PLAY

Multiply 9 by any number from 1 to 10, reverse the digits in your answer, and you'll have a new multiple of 9.

Multiply	Reverse the digits	New multiple of 9!
1 x 9 = 09	90	10 x 9 = 90
2 x 9 = 18	81	9 x 9 = 81
3 x 9 = 27	72	8 x 9 = 72
4 x 9 = 36	63	7 x 9 = 63
5 x 9 = 45	54	6 x 9 = 54
6 x 9 = 54	45	5 x 9 = 45
7 x 9 = 63	36	4 x 9 = 36
8 x 9 = 72	27	3 x 9 = 27
9 x 9 = 81	18	2 x 9 = 18
10 x 9 = 90	09	1 x 9 = 09

* * *

SMART MOUTHS

"Nobody can make you feel inferior without your permission."

—Eleanor Roosevelt

"I base most of my fashion taste on what doesn't itch."

—Gilda Radner

In a Yahoo poll, 82% of people thought females were more likely to use emoticons than males.

CRAZY DEFINITIONS GAME

Lots of people love making up funny new definitions for words. Some newspapers even hold contests for the best ones. Here are a few good ones we've found. Can you match each word with its wacky definition?

1. acute

2. avoidable

3. burglarize

4. catacomb

5. centipede

6. eyedropper

7. Erie Canal

8. finite

9. foul language

10. humbug

11. lunatic

12. mandate

13. relief

14. zinc

15. paradox

a. What a crook sees with

b. A clumsy ophthalmologist

c. A metric inchworm

d. Insect from the moon

e. Where you wash ze zaucepans

f. A rendezvous with a guy

g. Two physicians

h. A spooky waterway

i. A cockroach that forgot the words

j. What trees do in the spring

k. The opposite of an ugly

l. Good Sir Lancelot

m. What a bullfighter tries to do

n. Used for brushing cat hair

o. Cheep-cheep-cheep

ANSWERS: 1–k; 2–m; 3–a; 4–n; 5–c; 6–b; 7–h; 8–l; 9–o; 10–i; 11–d; 12–f; 13–j; 14–e; 15–g.

In Hong Kong, McDonald's serves its burgers between two rice patties instead of buns.

"E" IS FOR *EMMA*

Jane Austen is hot, hot, hot—her novels Pride and Prejudice, Sense and Sensibility, *and* Emma *are wildly popular again, thanks to lavish film versions starring the likes of Keira Knightley and Kate Winslet. Not bad for an author who wasn't even allowed to publish under her own name.*

HOME SCHOOL

Jane Austen was born December 16, 1775, in Steventon, Hampshire, England. The seventh of eight children and the younger of two girls, Jane was an avid reader who devoured books at a tremendous speed. Though she attended school only until the age of 11, her father, who came from a family of wealthy textile manufacturers, made sure she and her siblings had plenty to read and received a good education at home. The tight-knit, creative Austen family was known for writing and putting on their own plays, and when Jane was 12, she began filling notebooks with stories, poems, and observations. By the time she was 14, she had written her first book, *Love and Freindship*, a dark comedy parodying the novels of the time. (Yes, she misspelled "friendship." In her hurry to write things down, she often made spelling mistakes.)

UNLUCKY IN LOVE

As a young girl, Jane loved to dance and would wear out four pairs of dancing shoes in a year. Local gossips whispered that she was just "a silly, husband-hunting butterfly," but they were wrong. Though she had several suitors, Austen never married. She did have two close encounters with marriage, both of which seemed to be drawn straight from the pages of her books. First, at the age of 20, she fell in love with Tom Lefroy, the nephew of nearby neighbors. Unfortunately, Lefroy had no money to bring to the marriage and neither did Austen, so his family butted in and sent him away to London. Austen never saw him again.

A few years later, a wealthy friend of the family named Harris Bigg-Wither proposed to her. Austen said yes, but then withdrew her acceptance the next morning when she realized she didn't really care for her husband-to-be. As a result, Austen remained single for the rest of her life and lived in relative poverty. But she had no regrets: Years later, when a niece wrote to ask for advice on marriage, Austen told her, "I shall entreat you not to commit yourself further, and not to think of accepting him unless you really do like him. Anything is to be preferred or endured rather than marrying without affection."

POWER OF THE PEN

Because she was unmarried—and single women in the early 19th century had no way to support themselves—Austen always had to live with her relatives. Dressed in a cap and old clothes, she spent her days making breakfast for her family, practicing the piano, taking afternoon walks in the woods, and writing in the parlor. But if anyone came into the parlor, she tucked her pen and paper out of sight into her mahogany lap desk. Still, her writing didn't remain secret for long: In the four years from 1795 to 1799, Austen penned *Northanger Abbey*, *Sense and Sensibility*, *Mansfield Park*, and a book she called *First Impressions*. Little did she know that *First Impressions* would later become her most popular and enduring book—*Pride and Prejudice*—and its heroine, Elizabeth Bennet, would be one of the most admired women in literature. Austen didn't disagree: "I think her as delightful a creature as ever appeared in print." *Pride* was published in 1813 but, because writing novels was not considered a ladylike profession at the time, Austen's name didn't appear on the book. The title page read simply, "By a Lady."

LASTING INFLUENCE

Austen wrote several popular books, with *Emma* the last to be published during her lifetime. Austen herself wasn't sure how *Emma* would be received by the public, with "a heroine whom no one but myself will much like." She was wrong. Emma, the persistent matchmaker, was embraced by Austen's fans, and the story has been adapted many times for film, including the 1995 movie *Clueless*. (Another modern retelling of an Austen book is *Bridget Jones's Diary*, which is based on *Pride and Prejudice*.) Austen dedicated *Emma* to the Prince of Wales, who was a fan of her writing, though she wasn't particularly a fan of his. He asked her publisher if Austen (whom he knew only as the "Lady" from the title pages of her books) would dedicate *Emma* to him—and how do you turn down a prince?

A year after the publication of *Emma*, Jane Austen died, after a short illness, in her sister Cassandra's arms. She was only 41, and though her books had many devoted fans, they never earned enough money to make her rich or famous. In fact, it wasn't until after her death that the world finally learned the name of the "Lady" who wrote all those sensational novels.

AUSTEN MOVIE MARATHON

You may want to check out these movie adaptations of Jane Austen's books and life story.

- *Pride and Prejudice* (1995): This BBC miniseries, considered one of the best Austen adaptations, starred Jennifer Ehle as Elizabeth and made a star out of Colin Firth.
- *Sense and Sensibility* (1995) with Emma Thompson, Kate Winslet, and Hugh Grant
- *Emma* (1996) with Gwyneth Paltrow
- *Clueless* (1995) with Alicia Silverstone
- *Bridget Jones's Diary* (2001) with Renée Zellweger and Colin Firth
- *Bride and Prejudice* (2004): The Bollywood version, and great fun.
- *Pride and Prejudice* (2005) with Keira Knightley and Matthew Macfadyen
- *Lost in Austen* (2008): In this comedy, a modern-day Austen fan (Jemima Rooper) switches places with Elizabeth Bennet, the heroine of *Pride and Prejudice*.
- *Becoming Jane* (2007) with Anne Hathaway and James McAvoy, inspired by Austen's relationship with Tom Lefroy

Because their vocal cords are shorter, girls can talk for longer with less effort than boys.

I ENJOY BEING A GIRL

Being a girl can be a topsy-turvy experience. Celebrate it!

"I don't think of myself as a poor, deprived ghetto girl who made good. I think of myself as somebody who from an early age knew I was responsible for myself, and I had to make good."

—Oprah Winfrey

"It's the good girls who keep the diaries; bad girls never have the time."

—Tallulah Bankhead

"A girl should be two things: classy and fabulous."

—Coco Chanel

"I try to take one day at a time, but sometimes several days attack me all at once."

—artist Jennifer Yane

"Laugh and the world laughs with you. Cry and you cry with your girlfriends."

—author Laurie Kuslansky

"If you can't be a good example, then you'll have to be a terrible warning."

—writer Suzanne Braun Levine

"I'm not offended by all the dumb-blonde jokes because I know I'm not dumb…and I also know I'm not blonde."

—Dolly Parton

"Any girl can be glamorous. All you have to do is stand still and look stupid."

—actress Hedy Lamarr

FIONA GOES GEISHA

Meet Fiona Graham, the first and only Western woman to become a real Japanese geisha.

SO WHAT'S A GEISHA?

For many, the word *geisha* brings to mind a beautiful white-faced Japanese woman, dressed in an elaborate kimono, with perfectly lacquered black hair piled high on her head. That's how geishas looked nearly 400 years ago…and how they still look today. *Geisha* actually combines two words: *gei*, meaning "performing arts," and *sha*, meaning "person." In Japanese culture, geishas are highly trained musicians and dancers who treat everything they do as an art, from performing ancient tea ceremonies to engaging in witty conversation. Geishas entertain at exclusive teahouses and appear several times a year to do public performances. In the 1920s, the geisha business was thriving—there were 80,000 geishas in Japan. But today, there are only 2,000. So how did Fiona Graham, a girl from Australia, join this elite group of Japanese artists?

THE REAL LIFE

Fiona first visited Japan as a 15-year-old exchange student, and she liked it so much that she stayed and graduated from Tokyo's Keio Gijuku University. Then she moved to England to study documentary filmmaking and get her Ph.D in anthropology at Oxford University.

In 2005 she saw the film *Memoirs of a Geisha*—which, she felt, totally misrepresented the geisha culture. Determined to show the world the real life of a geisha, not the Western misrepresentation (which often portrays them as prostitutes), she decided to return to Japan to attend geisha school and make a documentary about it. Little did she realize that the decision would change her life.

GEISHA SCHOOL

Centuries ago, Japanese girls would begin training to be geishas at just three to five years old. But now girls usually start between the ages of 15 and 18 (and they, rather than their parents, choose it as their profession). The training is as rigorous as that of a professional ballerina or concert pianist—it involves many hours of work and a lot of discipline. Fiona first became a *maiko* (apprentice geisha) and lived with other *maikos* in a "geisha house," where they attended lessons.

Fiona was taught how to walk, talk, and dress properly and was required to master dancing and playing music. Each geisha has her own specific *gei* (art); Fiona's *gei* was playing a traditional bamboo flute called the *yokobue*. Becoming a geisha wasn't easy, and without her understanding of the Japanese language and culture, Graham says, it would have been impossible. She adds that a geisha's training is never really complete: "The older geishas attend lessons and practice on a daily basis into their 90s." But no one ever knows exactly how old they are because, following tradition, a geisha never reveals her age.

CALL ME SAYUKI

On December 19, 2007, Graham officially joined the 400-year-old vocation of the Japanese geisha when she made her debut as Sayuki (a Japanese name that means "transparent happiness"). Now she's the first and only foreigner to become a certified geisha. Other journalists and anthropologists have spent time observing and documenting the geisha, particularly American Liz Dalby, who spent several months in the 1970s living and working with geishas as research for her Ph.D. But no one besides Fiona Graham—now Sayuki—has made it her profession.

FLOWER AND WILLOW

Today Sayuki lives in Asakusa, Japan, and continues to work professionally as a geisha—a life that the

Japanese call "the flower and willow world." She's become quite well known, and even has a blog. She lectures at her alma mater, Keio Gijuku University, and also finds time for drawing anime and hiking...and occasionally slips out of her geisha outfits to relax in Western clothes. What does Sayuki love most about being a geisha? The kimonos. She owns a variety of handcrafted kimonos similar to the stunning powder-blue ensemble that she wore on the day of her debut. "I love performing, and I love wearing kimonos," Sayuki confessed to *Who* magazine. "Kimono shopping is absolutely addictive."

* * *

KARATE PRINCESS

Don't get in a fight with Her Highness Sheikha Maitha bint Mohammed Al Maktoum of Dubai, in the United Arab Emirates—she's an international karate and tae kwon do champ. After winning a silver medal in karate at the 2006 Asian Games, Sheikha Maitha was named the Arab world's best female athlete in 2007. At the 2008 Olympics, the 28-year-old princess was the first woman from the Persian Gulf region to carry her country's flag at the opening ceremony (which was a very big deal, since neighboring Saudi Arabia doesn't even allow women to be on its Olympic teams).

BADGE OF HONOR, FACE OF POOP

Geishas—the legendary, graceful women who have served as entertainers in Japan since the 1700s—developed their own beauty secrets over the centuries. Some were painful...and some were downright gross.

TOUGH BEAUTY

Being a geisha is hard on the body. Years of wearing their hair tightly wound, pulled, and shaped into the ideal geisha "do" often left the beautiful women with a small bald spot, recognized among the geishas as a "badge of honor." And if having an unsightly bald spot wasn't bad enough, applying loads of white makeup to achieve the perfect porcelain complexion caused many geisha women to suffer from chronic skin problems. To combat the effects of the makeup—which was, at one time, a toxic mix tinged with lead, zinc, or mercury—geisha turned to *uguisu no fun*, or bird-poop facials. Regular applications of nightingale poop not only helped remove makeup, but its natural enzymes and guanine helped soothe and heal skin.

If you're not the squeamish sort and you'd like to try one of these bird-poop facials, start saving your money. A few select spas offer them today, including one in New York where an *uguisu no fun* facial will cost you around $200.

ANIMAL CRACKERS

Q: What is a dog's favorite job? A: Rufferee!

Q: What do you get when you cross an elephant with an ant?

A: A dead ant.

Q: What did the farmer call the cow that had no milk?

A: An udder failure.

Q: Why do fish live in saltwater?

A: Because pepper makes them sneeze.

Q: What did the buffalo say to his son when he went away on a trip?

A: Bison!

Q: What did the judge say when the skunk walked into the courtroom?

A: "Odor in the court!"

Q: What do you get when you cross a snake and a pie?

A: A pie-thon!

Q: What do you get if you cross a skunk with a bear?

A: Winnie the Pee-yoo!

Q. How do you spot a high-tech spider?

A. He doesn't have a web, he has a website.

Q. What do you call an elephant at the North Pole?

A. Lost!

The trap-jaw ant can snap its jaws together at 145 mph, faster than any other animal.

PALM READING 101

Can you tell the future simply by studying the palm of your hand? For thousands of years, people have believed you can. It's fun...and now you can try it, too.

PALM PRIMER

Palmists—people who believe that the lines on our palms hold the keys to our personality and future—say that, like fingerprints, no two palms are the same. Each palm has its own unique life line, heart line, head line, fate line, fortune line, and health line. Palmists think that each of these lines tells a story of your past...and what your future may hold. Take a look at the chart and compare it to the palm of your dominant hand (the one you write with). Follow the guide and you, too, can become a palm reader.

THE LIFE LINE begins between the thumb and the forefinger and travels in an arc toward the wrist. It reflects the overall health of a person and the major life changes they've experienced, including significant injuries or illnesses. Contrary to popular belief, the length of the Life Line does not predict the length of life.

- Multiple Life Lines, or a long and deeply creased Life Line, indicates strength and vitality.
- A curvy Life Line reveals a person who is like the Energizer Bunny—full of get-up-and-go.
- Small loops in the Life Line are signs of major life

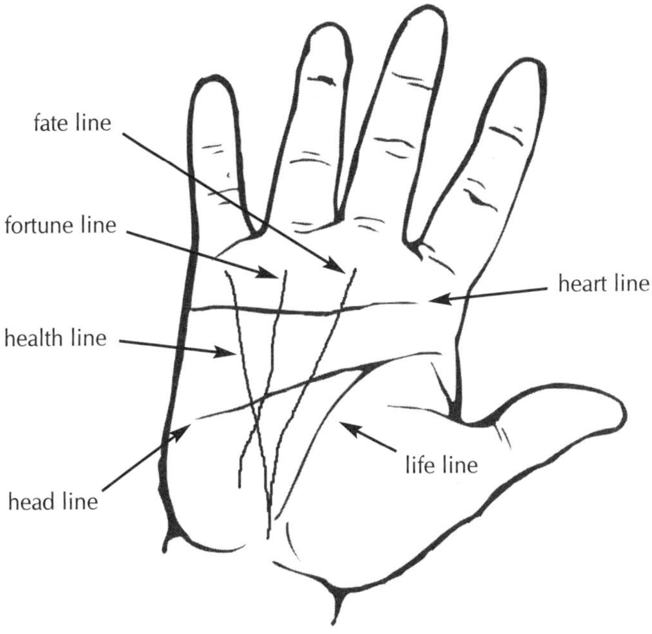

events like marriages and children—or significant illnesses or injuries, some of which may have required hospitalization.

- A break in the Life Line indicates a sudden change in lifestyle.
- Lines that cross the Life Line indicate troubles.

THE HEART LINE is a horizontal line that begins beneath the index finger or the middle finger (or between the two) and runs across to the edge of the palm, ending under the pinky finger. The Heart Line symbolizes emotional health and the potential for love and marriage.

...2 weeks in lakes and rivers, and a few days in the atmosphere.

- A long, broad Heart Line that begins beneath the index finger indicates a comfortable, easy love life.
- If the Heart Line is short, it may be a sign that the individual is not interested in love and marriage.
- When the Heart Line begins beneath the middle finger, this is a sign of a person who is focused on receiving love and has not yet matured into giving love.
- A Heart Line that begins between the index finger and the middle finger suggests an individual who tends to give her love away too easily.
- When the Heart Line is long and curves upward, this is an indication of someone who is naturally romantic.
- A straight Heart Line that runs parallel to the Head Line reveals strong emotional control.
- When the Heart Line is wavy and broken, or contains chains, this is a sign that there may be many love interests, but none of them will be very serious.
- A star on the Heart Line indicates happiness and bliss in marriage.
- Loops on the Heart Line indicate periods of heartbreak.
- If the Heart line contains small lines that extend upward, this symbolizes happiness. If the lines extend downward, this indicates disappointments.

THE HEAD LINE begins between the thumb and the forefinger and runs horizontally across the palm. This line indicates how a person approaches life, learning, and accomplishments.

Girls are more likely to be right-handed than boys are.

- When the Head Line is joined to the Life Line, this reveals an individual with a strong, logical mind who will not take unnecessary risks.
- A Head Line that is separated from the Life Line indicates enthusiasm for life and adventure.
- A short Head Line symbolizes a person who is very physically active, even to the point of taking life-threatening risks.
- When the Head Line curves down toward the wrist, this is a sign of a creative person.
- If the Head Line is wavy, the person may have a short attention span.
- A deep, long Head Line indicates a person who is a deep and imaginative thinker.

THE FATE LINE begins at the base of the palm and runs up the center toward the middle finger. The most important thing to note is that not everyone has a Fate Line. But if you do see one, it means the person's life may be affected by events beyond their control.

- A person without a Fate Line suggests that their life will probably be self-determined and predictable.
- A long, broad Fate Line points to a very interesting life that's heavily influenced by fate.
- A Fate Line that breaks and changes direction indicates at least one major career or life change.
- Small lines crossing the Fate Line indicate obstacles one may have to overcome in life.

First animated film ever nominated for a Best Picture Oscar: *Beauty and the Beast* (1991).

- Lines that branch down and away from the Fate Line reveal setbacks.
- Lines that branch up and away from the Fate Line show success in multiple areas of life.

THE FORTUNE LINE starts at the base of the hand and runs up toward the ring finger, parallel to the Fate Line. The Fortune Line symbolizes the path to success. Like the Fate Line, not everyone has a Fortune Line. If the Fortune Line is missing, this does not indicate a lack of success. The individual may become highly successful, but her success will likely be outside the public eye.

- A well-developed Fortune Line is a sign of satisfaction and success in life and work.
- More than one Fortune Line indicates more than one source of wealth.
- If the Fortune Line is broken or crossed by smaller lines, there will be stumbling blocks on the path to success.

- When the Fortune Line runs alongside the Life Line, it signifies an inheritance from a relative.
- When the fortune line starts near the Head Line, success will be enjoyed later in life—the fruit of a lifetime of work and saving.
- When the Fortune Line ends with a star or triangle beneath the ring finger, this is an indication that a brilliant career may be found in the field of fine arts or performing arts.

THE HEALTH LINE drops from below the pinky finger and runs diagonally across the palm to the base of the thumb. A hard-to-see Health Line is an indication of a healthy and strong individual. When the Health Line is long and easy to see, the individual's sense of health and well-being may be full of difficulties.

- A crooked Health Line indicates multiple health problems.
- A broken health line symbolizes digestive problems.
- Red lines crossing the Health Line indicate fevers.
- Little lines crossing the Health Line symbolize accidents.
- A loop on the Health Line indicates a significant health problem that may require hospitalization.
- A square on the Health Line is a sign of protection.
- If the Life, Head, and Health lines connect and create a triangle, this is considered the "lucky triangle"—the broader the triangle, the greater your luck.

Actress Tea Leoni's real name is Elizabeth Tea Pantleoni.

GODDESSES RULE: BENZAITEN

Japan's goddess of love, wealth, and talent is one lucky gal to know.

HAPPY NEW YEAR

Buddhists of Japan celebrate the Seven Gods of Good Fortune, deities who, according to legend, travel on their boat *Takarabune* ("Treasure Ship") every New Year's Eve to deliver gifts of talent, wealth, and fame to those humans worthy of their generosity. Only one of those Lucky Gods is female, and her name is Benzaiten. Benzaiten is not only beautiful, but she speaks poetry with every breath and charms the ear with each strum of her *biwa* (mandolin). According to legend, her eloquence is so powerful that once, when a dragon was terrorizing a village, she talked the beast into giving up its habit of eating children—and had to marry the dragon to get him to stop. But since she was the child of a dragon herself, she knew what she was getting into.

Benzaiten knows how to make an entrance: Her descent into the dragon's lair triggered an earthquake that caused the island of Enoshima to emerge from the sea. Her followers have tended temples on that island for more than 1,000 years. She sometimes appears to humans in the shape of a snake (her favorite creature), which is why, even today, the Japanese consider it good luck to carry a little piece of snakeskin in their wallet.

CAUTION: PARENTS TEXTING

More examples of parents trying to be cool while they're texting their kids. (And then their kids turned them in by posting these on the internet.)

Dad: mt dishwasher!

Me: Mount Dishwasher?

Dad: No, empty dishwasher, I was being cool.

Mom: We R eating soup.

Mom: We R walking.

Mom: We R home.

Me: you dont have to capitalize the r…

Mom: Can you please call me when you need to be picked up! Don't do anything stupid! :-)8

Me: What is that emoticon?

Mom: bowtie man! He doesn't do anything stupid

Mom: :D (y)

Me: What is that supposed to be

Mom: I'm very happy plus thumbs up

Dad: R U H Y

Me: WHAT?!

Dad: R U Home Yet

Me: Yes, dad.

Dad: thats the bombdiggity

Mom: W r u

Me: Umm… Where am I? Downtown

Mom: W u d

Me: Hanging out with people…

Mom: W t u c h

Me: WHAT?

Mom: What time u coming home

Dad: A crisp autumn breeze rustles through the colorful trees of Maryland on a sunny November day, beckoning you home.

Me: beautiful diction dad

Dad: Haha thx. How r u>?

Sharks have existed for at least 300 million years—since before the dinosaurs.

WHO'S AFRAID OF 13?

Ever have a really bad day? Some people think they're caused by the number 13, and they'll go to extreme lengths to avoid it.

PEOPLE

- Henry Ford, the inventor of the auto assembly line, would not do business on Friday the 13th.
- President Franklin Delano Roosevelt would not dine in a group of 13 people.
- Horror novelist Stephen King said, "When I'm reading, I will not stop on page 94, page 193, or page 382. The digits of these numbers add up to 13."

THINGS

- Airline flights are never numbered 13. Airports never have a gate 13. There is no 13th row on most airplanes.
- In 2007 Brussels Airlines painted a new logo on all of its planes with the B spelled out in 13 dots. When passengers refused to fly the "unlucky" planes, the company added a 14th dot to the logo.
- Most hotels do not have a 13th floor or a room 13.
- At California's Santa Anita racetrack, the horse stalls are numbered 12, 12A and 14.
- In 2009 a 13-story building in Shanghai, China, simply fell over.

RANDOM FACTS ABOUT 13

- Many cities have a 12th Street, then a street with a name, and then a 14th Street.
- Italians never include the number 13 in their national lottery.
- In 1970 the *Apollo 13* moon mission launched on April 11th at 13:13 (1:13 p.m.) Central time—on purpose, as a play on the "unlucky" number of the mission. On April 13th, one of the spacecraft's oxygen tanks exploded, and the lives of all three crew members were instantly in peril. The good news? Though the mission failed, the astronauts made it home alive.

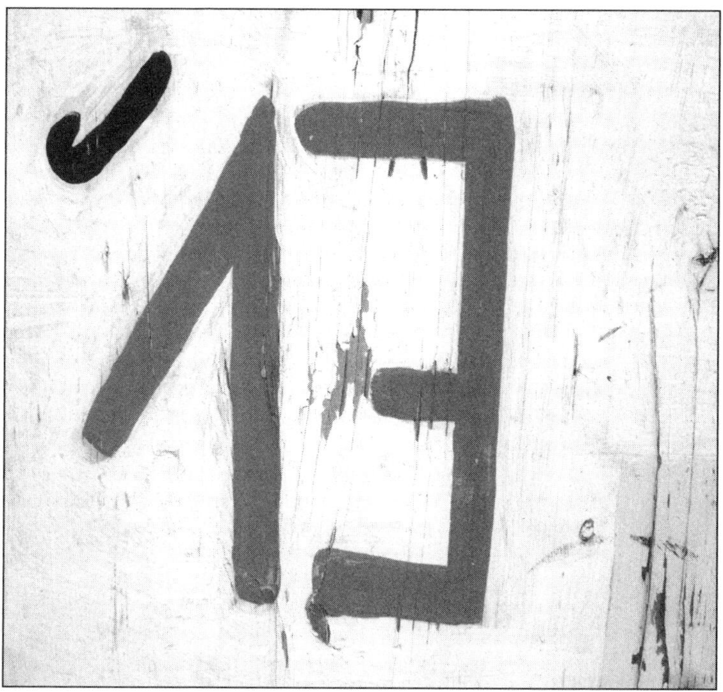

YOU GO, GIRL!

At a time when "proper" ladies were wearing hoopskirts and serving tea in their parlors, this crackerjack newspaper journalist was out chasing stories. *(For more "go girls," turn to pages 121 and 169.)*

ACE REPORTER

Born in 1769, Anne Newport Royall moved to Washington, D.C., in the early 1800s. Her husband, a Revolutionary War veteran, had recently died, and she needed to make a living, so she took up writing. She started out with travel stories, and later put her energy into editing her own newspaper, *The Huntress*. Within a few years, she'd developed a reputation for exposing political corruption and religious fraud.

THE BARE FACTS

Royall's determination to hunt down news became the stuff of legend. According to one story, on a morning in 1830, she came upon President John Quincy Adams skinny-dipping in the Potomac River (presidents could do that back then). Instead of blushing and turning away, Royall sat down on Adams's clothes and refused to budge until he agreed to grant her an exclusive interview.

Over her lifetime, Anne Royall gained a reputation for speaking out in print against government waste, crooked politicians, and injustices to Native Americans. She continued to write books and publish articles until her death in 1854 at the age of 85.

WACKY HEADLINES

Here's something we never get tired of: head-scratching bloopers from real newspapers. Can you figure out what they were trying to say?

PLENTY DO DO HERE FOR LOCAL TOURISTS

SHORTAGE OF BRAINS SLOWS MEDICAL RESEARCH

POLICEMAN SHOOTS MAN WITH KNIFE

EYE DROPS OFF SHELF

MATERIAL IN DIAPERS COULD HELP MAKE THE DESERTS BLOOM

SCHOOL BANS ALL KINDS OF NUTS ON CAMPUS

ASTRONAUT TAKES BLAME FOR GAS IN SPACECRAFT

SOMETHING WENT WRONG IN JET CRASH, EXPERT SAYS

DRUNK GETS NINE MONTHS IN VIOLIN CASE

LINGERIE SHIPMENT HIJACKED—THIEF GIVES POLICE THE SLIP

COMMISSIONER DAVIS TO HEAD "ASSAULT ON LITERACY MONTH"

RED TAPE HOLDS UP NEW BRIDGE

PATIENT AT DEATH'S DOOR—DOCTORS PULL HIM THROUGH

At age 18, the future Queen Elizabeth II served as a mechanic in the British military.

EIGHT STEPS TO POP-STAR SUCCESS

How do you become a megastar? If you're multiplatinum-selling R&B singer Rihanna from the Caribbean island of Barbados, it's simple: You start young and charge straight up the ladder of success.

Step 1: Start by watching Beyoncé in all of the Destiny's Child videos, and imitate every move she makes.

Step 2: When your school holds a talent show, sing Mariah Carey's "Hero" and knock your classmates' socks off.

Step 3: Enter a high-school beauty pageant at 15—and win.

Step 4: Find out that famed music producer Evan Rogers is vacationing on your island, and have a friend get you a private audition with him.

Step 5: When Rogers goes crazy for your singing and invites you to New York City to record a demo—go!

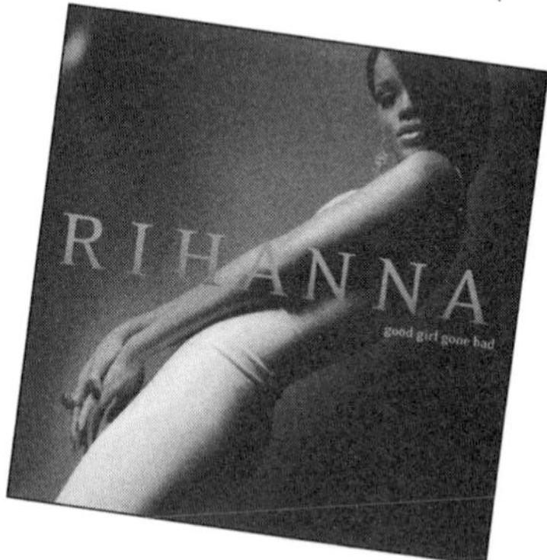

Step 6: When Rogers passes your demo to Jay-Z of Def Jam records, and Jay-Z also wants you to audition, sing Whitney Houston's "For the Love of You" for him.

Step 7: When Jay-Z signs you to a contract that day, record your first single, "Pon de Replay."

Step 8: Watch your first single go straight to the top of the pop charts. Presto! At 17, you're a star.

SIX FACTS ABOUT RIHANNA

1. "RiRi," as the press likes to calls her, currently sports 13 tattoos.
2. Since 2005 she's had 150 different hairstyles.
3. Her dad is from Barbados, and her mom is from Guyana, in South America.
4. What does Rihanna miss most about her home in Barbados? Her mom's cooking. Fave foods are callaloo soup (callaloo is a leafy spinach-type plant also known as amaranth) and jerk chicken ("jerk" is a way of barbecuing meat with a tangy rub of herbs and spices).
5. She holds the honorary title of "Ambassador for Culture and Youth" for her native Barbados.
6. She is one of only four artists who've had six number-one singles on the pop charts. (The other three? Mariah Carey, Lady Gaga, and Beyoncé.)

STAR QUALITY

Lots of pop hopefuls are talented, but the quality that pushed Rihanna to the top was what music people like to call that special "something." As Jay-Z told *Rolling Stone*, "I knew within two minutes that Rihanna was a star."

WORD PUZZLES

Try to figure out the word or phrase that each puzzle represents. (For example: WONALICEDERLAND means "Alice in Wonderland.")

1. NA NA FISH

2. ABCDEFGHIJKLMN
OPQRSTVWXYZ

3. MAN
BOARD

4. VISION VISION

5. C
YOURSELF
YOURSELF
YOURSELF
YOURSELF

6. SUGAR
x SUGAR
x SUGAR

7. __________IT

8. DEATH LIFE

9. O_ER_T_O_

10. LILASTNE

11. SYMPHON

12. T _ R N

13. STEP SPETS SPETS

14. FUNNY FUNNY
WORDS WORDS
WORDS WORDS

15. VA DERS

Solutions: 1. Tuna fish (two na fish); 2. Missing you (u); 3. Man overboard; 4. Double vision; 5. See fo(u)r yourself; 6. Sugar cube(d); 7. Blanket; 8. Life after death; 9. Painless operation; 10. Last in line; 11. Unfinished symphony; 12. No U-Turn; 13. One step forward, two steps backward; 14. Too (2) funny for (4) words; 15. Space Invaders.

Cleopatra became the ruler of Egypt at age 18.

CHOCOLATE SPA

Spas across America are offering chocolate wraps, chocolate facials, chocolate eyebrow waxes, and chocolate pedicures. Why? Because chocolate isn't just good for your insides—it also softens and renews your outsides. Give these beautylicious recipes a try and judge for yourself.

CHOCOLATE FACIAL

Ingredients:

⅓ cup unsweetened cocoa powder
3 tablespoons heavy cream
2 teaspoons cottage cheese
¼ cup honey
1 tablespoon oatmeal powder (finely ground oatmeal)

Instructions:

1. Mix all ingredients together in a bowl.
2. Spread the mixture on your face.
3. Relax for 10 minutes and "feel the heal."
4. Use a warm, moist washcloth to remove the chocolate paste; apply moisturizer.

CHOCOLATE LIP BALM

Ingredients:

3 tablespoons cocoa butter
3–4 chocolate chips
¼ teaspoon olive oil or almond oil
1 vitamin E capsule

In the 12th century, Queen Isabeau of France used a face cream made of pig brains.

Instructions:

1. Put cocoa butter in a small, microwave-safe dish and melt in a microwave.

2. Add chocolate chips and stir until melted; continue to microwave as needed.

3. Squeeze in the vitamin E oil from the capsule, and add olive or almond oil.

4. Stir the mixture very well.

5. Put in a small, clean, airtight container and let cool. Apply to lips as needed.

CHOCOLATE MILK BATH MIX

Ingredients:

2 cups powdered milk
¼ cup cocoa powder
2 tablespoons cornstarch
pinch of cinnamon (optional)

Instructions:

1. Mix all ingredients together and transfer the mixture to a glass or shaker jar.

2. While filling the tub, sprinkle as much of the chocolate bath mix as you'd like.

3. Stir the water to dissolve.

4. Soak and inhale the delicious aroma of chocolate.

☆ STARSTRUCK, PART II ☆

On page 157, we took you on a spin through the first six signs of the zodiac. Here, last but not least, are the rest—from the scales of justice to the scales of fishes. Which one are you?

♎ LIBRA (September 23–October 22)

Element: Air
Ruling Planet: Venus
Gemstone: Opal
Symbol: Scales of Justice
Scent: Orange

Flower: Bluebell
Lucky Numbers: 7, 8, 10, 27
Ice Cream: Ben & Jerry's Imagine Whirled Peace

Peacekeeper. You, Ms. Libra, are first and foremost a real charmer. People like you because you are also an honest and trustworthy team player and friend. Your natural diplomacy helps you to stay fair and balanced, because you are able to weigh both sides of a problem. But your desire to keep the peace can keep you on the fence too long, when your friends are begging you to take sides. Be bold. Make choices.

Famous Libra Women: Ashanti, Avril Lavigne, Serena Williams, Ursula K. Le Guin, Martina Navratilova

♏ SCORPIO (October 23–November 21)

Element: Water
Ruling Planet: Mars
Gemstone: Topaz
Symbol: Scorpion
Scent: Forest essences

Flower: Geranium
Lucky Numbers: 7, 11, 23, 47
Ice Cream: Häagen-Dazs Mocha Almond Fudge

Force of Nature. Scorpios are practically on fire with passion for love and life. You adore mysteries, secrets, and anything magical. You are wise beyond your years, so much so that it can be very awkward for you—especially when you are young. You have an uncanny ability to understand your friends' deepest desires, and you wish they could understand yours. Stay positive and focused. When you channel your amazing energy, there's nothing you can't achieve.

Famous Scorpio Women: Anne Hathaway, Katy Perry, k.d. lang, Hillary Clinton, Whoopi Goldberg

♐ SAGITTARIUS (November 22–December 20)

Element: Fire
Ruling Planet: Jupiter
Gemstone: Turquoise
Symbol: The Archer
Scent: All flowers

Flower: Carnation
Lucky Numbers: 3, 5, 9, 14, 37
Ice Cream: Ben & Jerry's Everything But The…

Ms. Adventure. As a fun-loving Sagittarius, you keep your Jeep packed with skis, climbing ropes, a skateboard, and your trusty Golden Retriever. "Let's do it!" is your battle cry. Your biggest fear? Boredom. This can lead to a restlessness that inspires unsafe pranks and makes you a little too much of a party girl. You are smart, funny, and great at solving complicated problems, but you can be a bit absentminded. Here's a tip: For your next adventure, make sure you pack *all* your gear.

Most MTV Music Awards: Madonna, with 20.

Famous Sagittarius Women: Scarlett Johansson, Britney Spears, Lucy Liu, Jane Austen, Tyra Banks, Diane Sawyer

♑ CAPRICORN (December 21–January 19)

Element: Earth
Ruling Planet: Saturn
Gemstone: Garnet
Symbol: The Goat
Scent: Lavender

Flower: Pansy
Lucky Numbers: 2, 8, 28, 47
Ice Cream: Häagen-Dazs Rocky Road

Overachiever. As a Capricorn girl, once you've made up your mind to do something, you're like a Zen master. And a Zen master knows two things: 1) The first step to the top of the mountain is the hardest step, and 2) Every step is the first step. So what if it takes 10,000 first steps? You're on your way. But you can be so intent on your goal that you forget everything else. Let a friend take the lead every now and then…you'll still get to the top.

Famous Capricorn Women: Janis Joplin, Dolly Parton, Zooey Deschanel, Stephenie Meyer

♒ AQUARIUS (January 20–February 18)

Element: Air
Ruling Planet: Uranus
Gemstone: Amethyst
Symbol: The Water Bearer
Scent: Incense

Flower: Orchid
Lucky Numbers: 2, 4, 10, 39, 49
Ice Cream: Häagen-Dazs Green Tea

Super Sleuth. Ms. Aquarius, you are a detective, inventor, scientist, and peacemaker, all rolled into one amazing girl. If there's a mystery, you've got the mental tools to solve it. You are a student of life who rarely—if ever—suffers from boredom. But you tend to doubt yourself and wonder if your ideas are worth sharing. They are. Be brave and put yourself out there.

Famous Aquarius Women: Oprah Winfrey, Meg Cabot, Shakira, E. L. Konigsburg, Jennifer Aniston, Yoko Ono

♓ PISCES: February 19–March 19

Element: Water
Ruling Planet: Neptune
Gemstone: Bloodstone
Symbol: The Fishes
Scent: Pure floral essences

Flower: Water Lily
Lucky Numbers: 2, 4, 11, 24, 32
Ice Cream: Ben & Jerry's Phish Food

BFF. As the last sign in the zodiac, you, Ms. Pisces, have integrated all the other signs within you. You are compassionate, artistic, funny, smart, and shy, and make the perfect best friend. You are a natural healer and humanitarian. Too often, you put everyone else first and blame yourself when something goes wrong. Celebrate your talents and use your imagination to follow your own dreams.

Famous Pisces Women: Queen Latifah, Drew Barrymore, Erykah Badu, Anaïs Nin, Amy Tan

In one poll, 34% of moms admitted that they hated the name of a friend's baby.

HORSE SENSE

Amaze your horse-loving friends with these cool facts!

- Horses have the largest eyes of any land mammal.
- Horses can't vomit.
- Horses sleep only 3–4 hours in a 24-hour period.
- A horse can poop up to 15 times a day!
- If you're at a horse show and you see a horse with a red ribbon on its tail—stay back! That ribbon means he kicks.
- On May 28, 2003, a Haflinger filly named Prometea became the first horse clone to be born. She was cloned by scientists in Italy.
- Legend has it that the Arabian horse was created by Allah out of "a handful of the southern wind."
- The names Philip and Philipa mean "lover of horses."

"There is something about riding down the street on a prancing horse that makes you feel like something, even when you ain't a thing."

—Will Rogers, humorist (1879–1935)

In 1854 Cadbury became the official chocolate supplier to Queen Victoria of England.

CODE RED!

You've got an awesome weekend planned...and suddenly a zit appears. What should you do? How about trying some of these old-time home remedies?

JUICE 'EM

Attack those blemishes with radish-seed juice. Boil 2 tablespoons of radish seeds in 4 cups of distilled water for 10 minutes. Let cool completely. To help diminish the appearance of blackheads and zits, soak a clean cloth in the radish juice and gently apply to your skin. This works best if you use it on a regular basis. The cooling, antiseptic qualities of radish juice can also be used on insect bites.

SPOT ON

Try zapping those zits with a dab of white, non-fluoride, non-tartar-control toothpaste and let dry. You might feel a little tingling—that's the toothpaste drying out your zit. But if it burns, wash the toothpaste off right away—your skin may be too sensitive for it.

EGG ON YOUR FACE

Wipe out major breakouts with a complete egg-and-corn-flour facial. Mix a tablespoon of corn flour with an egg white. Smooth over the breakout area. Let dry, then rinse off with warm water. The mixture acts like a sponge, soaking up the oils from your skin.

GHOST GIRLS OF TEXAS

What is it about the state of Texas and ghosts? Here are a few spirited ladies who seem to love the state so much that they refuse to leave it…ever.

GOOD-LUCK CHARM

Texas Wesleyan University in Fort Worth has been around since 1890, but it took a century for a ghost to make an appearance on campus. In the early 1990s, students rehearsing school plays said that they'd seen a woman, dressed in 1890s clothes, sitting in the back of the theater and staring at the stage. If anyone called out to her, she didn't answer but just kept looking straight ahead. Then, as soon as they went back to rehearsing, she'd move, or cough, or make a noise. At first everyone was creeped out by this ghostly guest, but then they noticed a curious phenomenon: Whenever the ghost (whom the students named "Georgia") showed up in rehearsals, that show was a monster hit. Who was she? A local ghost expert thinks "Georgia" might be the spirit of Sarah Dobkins, who died in 1896 on the grounds where the university now stands.

THE BRIDE GOES SHOPPING

Late one night several years ago, two women staying at the Hotel Driskill in Austin decided to snoop around the hotel's fourth floor, which was closed for renovations. As they were walking down the supposedly abandoned hall, the elevator opened and a stylish young woman, carrying an armful of shopping bags, got out and went into Room 29. The next day, the women mentioned the incident to the desk clerk, who said, "That's impossible." Then, to prove it, he took them up to Room 29. The walls were covered with plastic, and there was no bed or sink. "You've just seen the Houston Bride," the clerk told them. Who was she? A socialite who was jilted by her fiancé in 1990. She committed suicide in Room 29 after going on a wild shopping spree using her ex-boyfriend's credit cards. Ever since, hotel guests have occasionally claimed that they've seen her come out of the elevator and go into Room 29, her arms full of packages.

CREEPY CUSTODIAN

Room 331 in the biology building of Texas Tech University in Lubbock has a carpeted floor. What's unusual about that? The carpet's there to hide a bloodstain that won't go away. That's eerie enough…but not nearly as weird as the ghostly face of a woman that students say they've seen peeking into the classrooms during exams. She shakes her head as if deeply disappointed by what she sees, then moves away. Some say the ghost is Sarah Morgan, a custodian who was brutally murdered in 1967 when she surprised a student trying to steal the answers for a big exam. The guy panicked and killed her with a medical scalpel, and she was found slumped in a pool of blood. According to local lore, every year on the anniversary of her murder, the stain on the floor in Room 331 grows as wet and dark as the day she was killed.

PROPER SEASONING

Three hundred years ago, the British solved the dilemma of how to get the right girl to meet the right boy. How? With an event called "the Season." It still exists today.

THE SEASON

In England during the 18th and 19th centuries, when an upper-class young lady reached 17, she was considered eligible for marriage. It was also time to introduce her to society during the "social season"—a four-month period each year when everybody who was anybody left their country estates and went to London to see and be seen. The Season lasted from April to August and was filled with parties, dances, concerts, and operas, providing numerous opportunities for young people to meet.

COMING OUT

For a young *debutante* (French for "beginner"), her introduction to society, or "coming out," was one of the most important moments of her life: This was her chance to make a good impression and, hopefully, find a suitable husband. If it didn't happen in her first year, she had only one or two years to get herself a guy. After that, she passed into spinsterhood (at the ripe old age of 20), and would have little hope of finding a mate.

Preparations for the Season were intense, and wealthy families spent fortunes on the perfect clothing and hairstyles for their daughters. The Season began with the debutante's nerve-shattering formal presentation at Buckingham Palace, where she promenaded in a spectacular gown past everyone who mattered and then curtseyed before the queen or king. Once she survived that presentation, the "deb" was ready to party hardy!

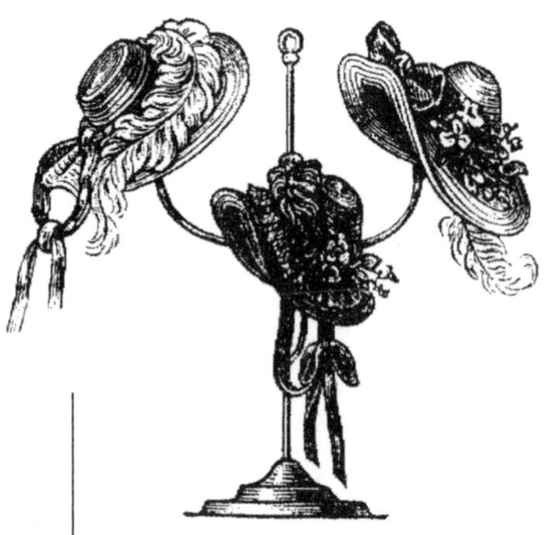

DAY BY DAY

For a debutante during the Season, every day but Sunday was packed with activities. Here's what a typical day might look like:

9 a.m.: Rise and shine—and get dressed.

11 a.m.: Attend a breakfast party.

Noon: Ride in the park or attend an art exhibition.

2 p.m.: Luncheon.

3 p.m.: Attend afternoon concert or make formal calls.

4 p.m.: Attend tea party or garden party.

5 p.m.: Ride or walk through the park.

7 p.m.: Dinner.

8 p.m.: Attend opera or theater.

10 p.m.: Attend reception or soiree.

Midnight to 5 a.m.: Attend ball or three or four parties—chaperoned, of course.

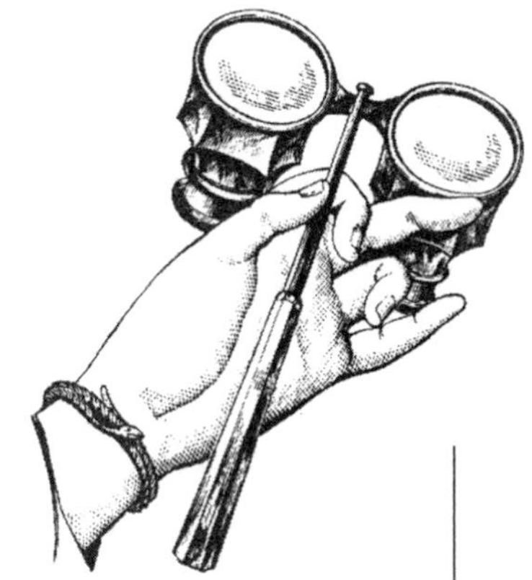

SEASONS OF CHANGE

You may think it's an antiquated practice, but the Season still exists in London today, though "debs" are no longer presented at court. However, they're still expected to attend key events such as the Royal Ascot horse race and the Chelsea Flower Show. At the Henley Royal Regatta boat race, princesses, duchesses, and wealthy young ladies promenade before society in all their glory, wearing enormous hats. (The hats are part of the social dress code—ladies *have* to wear them.) Not only are hats required at the Royal Regatta, but ladies' hem lengths are also strictly enforced—they must be below the knee. If there is any question about the length, the hem is measured by an official, and if it's found to be too short, the lady is ejected from the event.

...to make room for women's tall, elaborate hairdos, fashionable at the time.

GROANERS, PART II

More jokes that are so bad...they're good.

Q: What do you call a bear with no ear?

A: B.

Q: Why do toadstools grow so close together?

A: They don't need mushroom.

Q: What is an archaeologist?

A: Someone whose career is in ruins.

Q: If two's company and three's a crowd, what are four and five?

A: Nine.

Q: What did one toilet say to the other toilet?

A: You look a little flushed.

Q: Why did the student eat his homework?

A: The teacher told him it was a piece of cake.

Q: Why do elephants never forget?

A: Because nobody ever tells them anything.

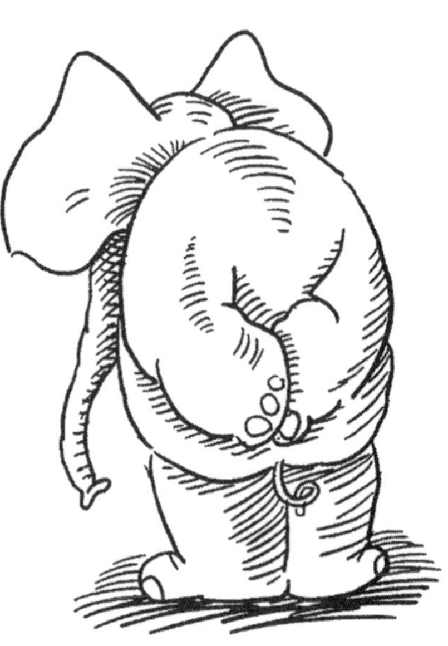

GODDESSES RULE: ATHENA

Here's the next in our series of "biographies" from the days when goddesses ruled: Meet Athena, the Greek goddess of wisdom...and war.

DON'T MESS WITH THE GODDESS

To the ancient Greeks, Athena was one of the most powerful of all goddesses (it didn't hurt that she was the daughter of Zeus, king of the gods). Smart and beautiful, she was the goddess of wisdom. But Athena was also a master of the martial arts, which made her the goddess of war, too. In statues and paintings, she was often shown with an owl (an ancient symbol of wisdom) on her shoulder and a serpent around her wrist (the snake represented Erichthonius, an early Greek king whom Athena had protected). This wonder woman had many talents, including pottery, gardening, and weaving. When a famed weaver named Arachne claimed that her work was better than Athena's, the angry goddess challenged her to a contest. Athena lost—and was so angry that she turned the weaver into a spider. According to the legend, that's why spiders are called *arachnids* today.

DIVINE GIFTS

That wasn't the only contest Athena got caught up in.

Poseidon, god of the sea, became jealous of Athena's popularity with the Greeks, so he proposed another challenge for her: Each of them would make a fabulous gift and give it to the people of Greece. Whoever's gift was more popular would become the patron god of a new Greek city. Poseidon went first. Knowing how important water was to a community, he gave the city a well. "Now you'll have water forever," he boasted. Not so fast—Poseidon's well was full of undrinkable saltwater. Wise goddess that she was, Athena gave the Greeks a perfect gift, one that would keep on giving: an olive tree. It would provide shade from the sun, oil for lamps, and food for the table. Her gift won, and the new city was named Athens in her honor. Ever since, the olive branch has been considered a universal symbol of friendship, generosity, and peace.

THE PRINCESS DIARIES, PART II: HAPPILY EVER AFTER?

Not all princes and princesses enjoy fairy-tale endings. Check out these real-life stories.

Marie Antoinette of Austria (1755–93) + Louis XVI of France (1754–93)

When Marie Antoinette was just 14 years old, she was declared the most beautiful princess in Europe. But did she get to choose her prince? No way. Her parents, the emperor and empress of Austria, forced her to marry the future King Louis XVI of France—an overweight, painfully shy 15-year-old. Instead of appreciating his beautiful young bride, Louis avoided her like the plague and preferred to spend his time working on his lock collection and riding his horse on hunting expeditions. This made it difficult for Marie Antoinette to have children, the number-one job of a queen at that time. Left on her own, Queen Marie Antoinette amused herself by throwing lavish parties and spending endless amounts of money on dinners, dances, and beautiful gowns (every six months, she ordered 36 new ones). And her huge powdered wigs were the stuff of legend: Topped with figurines, fruit, and model ships, they nearly always sported

ostrich plumes three feet high. Naturally, France's starving peasants were not too happy about their queen's spending habits, and an angry mob finally stormed the palace in 1792. The French Revolution was in full force, and Louis and Marie Antoinette's reign was over. On October 16, 1793, Marie Antoinette, wearing her purple silk slippers, climbed the steps of the guillotine and was beheaded.

Caroline Mathilde of Great Britain (1751–75) + Christian VII of Denmark (1749–1808)

Caroline Mathilde was 15 when she discovered something was really rotten in Denmark: It was Christian, her 17-year-old alcoholic cousin, whom she'd been sent there to marry. Extremely frail and short (his head barely reached Caroline's shoulder), Christian was also prone to violent fits of temper. When he wasn't banging his

head until blood gushed out or smashing up the furniture in his own house, he was on the streets of Copenhagen with his gang of friends, beating innocent people with spiked clubs. He loved public trials and often staged mock executions of his friends, flogging them until they bled. His insane behavior made Caroline miserable, and she turned to her husband's doctor for comfort and affection. Bad idea: She was thrown in prison and eventually deported to England. Her boyfriend was also arrested, but he didn't fare so well: His right hand was cut off, and then his head. Afterward, his body was drawn and quartered. (Ew.)

Maria Anna of Italy (1803–84) + Ferdinand I of Austria (1793–1875)

Maria Anna married Archduke Ferdinand I when she was 28 and he was 38. Ferdinand's parents were double first cousins (meaning they shared the same great-grandparents), and the inbreeding left him with many physical problems. He was born with water on the brain, which gave him a huge head, and he suffered from a shrunken body and severe epilepsy. Ferdinand also had the famous "Hapsburg jaw" (see page 68) and his tongue was too large for his mouth, which made it hard for him to talk. By all accounts, the only understandable sentence he ever spoke was to his cook: "I'm the king and I want dumplings!" He was so dim-witted that his favorite activity was shoving his bottom in a wastebasket and rolling around the floor. But that didn't stop Ferdinand from being crowned emperor of Austria. (Though his father had made sure that Ferdinand's advisors would really run the country.) It also didn't stop Maria Anna from becoming lovingly devoted to him. After ruling the Austrian Empire for 18 years, Ferdinand was finally pushed aside to let his nephew, Franz Joseph, rule. Maria Anna and Ferdinand spent the rest of their happily-ever-after puttering around a castle in the city of Prague.

FLAPPER TALK

If you lived in the Roaring Twenties, you might have a been a "flapper"—a rebellious girl who bobbed her hair, wore short skirts, listened to jazz, and even (gasp!) drove a car. And flappers had a language all their own. Here's a sample.

• "Everything's copacetic!"
Everything's great!

• "Hot diggity dog!"
I'm so excited!

• "He says I'm the cat's pajamas."
He thinks I'm the best.

• "My jazzbo."
My boyfriend.

• "He says I've got nice gams and I'm his Sheba."
He says I have nice legs and I'm beautiful.

• "He's a real sheik."
He's a total hottie.

• "What's up, Jellybean?"
(That's how a flapper greets her jazzbo.)

• "This place is swanky."
This place is high-class.

• "Watch out for Charlie; he's pretty hard-boiled."
He's a tough guy—cool and unsentimental.

• "We're pretty stuck on each other."
We like each other.

• "He's a real snuggle-pup." *He likes to do a lot of hugging.*

• "He goes in for heavy necking."
He likes to do a lot of kissing, too.

• "He's a real flat tire."
He's a bore.

• "She is one dumb Dora."
She isn't very bright.

• "He drank so much giggle water he was ossified!" *He drank too much and got drunk.*

• "The two-timer ran out on me!"
He started dating another girl.

• "Go fly a kite!"
Get away from me!

• "Lulu still carries a torch for him."
Lulu's still in love with him.

• "We spent all night beating our gums."
We talked the whole time.

• "She'll find a sugar daddy."
She'll find someone to take care of her.

• "Ab-so-lute-ly pos-a-tute-ly." *I agree.*

• "Put your glad rags on."
Wear your best outfit.

• "Hot socks!" *Great!*

• "He's a real lounge lizard."
He's a ladies' man who hangs out at clubs.

• "He's the cat's meow!"
He's the best thing ever.

• "You slaughter me!"
You make me laugh.

• "That was some ritzy party. And thanks for the buggy ride."
Great party. Thanks for the car ride home.

Technically, only female falcons are called *falcons*; males are called *tiercels*.

RECIPE FOR BEAUTY

Here's a shampoo you can make at home that will leave your hair smelling great...and can save you a bundle.

PEPPERMINT-CHAMOMILE SHAMPOO

With this simple recipe, you can make your own minty herbal shampoo.

Ingredients

1 cup water

3 bags chamomile tea

3 bags peppermint tea

2 tablespoons liquid Castile soap

1 teaspoon light vegetable oil

Instructions

1. Bring water to a boil.
2. Steep all six tea bags for 20 minutes.
3. Let cool to room temperature.
4. Remove tea bags.
5. Add Castile soap and vegetable oil to brewed tea and stir well.
6. Store in an airtight container at room temperature.

To Use

Massage palm-sized amount into hair and scalp. Rinse well.

YOU NAME IT

One of our BRI authors has a strange hobby: inventing punny names for characters in his stories. Here are a few of our favorites. Can you think of more?

Raven Lunatic

Dawn Zerlylight

Jane Linkfence

Jen Rummy

Scarlett Fever

Nan Egote

Pam Purd

Kay Turring

Marsha Ninvaders

Kristol Vace

Jan Ator

Sue Mohressler

Dinah Sore

Dinah Stee

Ella Mentry

Lena Little-Closer

Tara Daktuhl

Belle Jumm

Allie Katz

Bev Ridge

Tess Tube

Fawn Dove Chocklut

Parma Zhan

Eva Looshun

Kat Burglur

Paula Nashun

Beth Lee Hamm

Bea Keaper

Anna Graham

Farrah Sweel

America's first policewoman, Alice Wells (1909), designed her own uniform.

FAMOUS LAST WORDS

Every good book has a good finish, and that includes its very last words. How many of these have you read?

"It is not often that someone comes along who is a true friend and a good writer. Charlotte was both."

—***Charlotte's Web***

"The scar had not pained Harry for nineteen years. All was well."

—***Harry Potter and the Deathly Hallows***

"You're off to great places! Today is your day! Your mountain is waiting. So…get on your way!"

—***Oh, the Places You'll Go!***

"Oh, my girls, however long you may live, I never can wish you a greater happiness than this!"

—***Little Women***

"I'm so glad to be at home again."

—***The Wonderful Wizard of Oz***

"But they never learned what it was that Mrs. Whatsit, Mrs. Who, and Mrs. Which had to do, for there was a gust of wind, and they were gone."

—***A Wrinkle in Time***

"But I reckon I got to light out for the Territory ahead of the rest, because Aunt Sally she's going to adopt me and sivilize me and I can't stand it. I been there before."

—***The Adventures of Huckleberry Finn***

"I take his hand, holding tightly, preparing for the cameras, and dreading the moment when I will finally have to let go."

—***The Hunger Games***

"So much of life in its meshes! She called in her soul to come and see."

—***Their Eyes Were Watching God***

"It is a far, far better thing that I do, than I have ever done; it is a far, far better rest that I go to, than I have ever known."

—***A Tale of Two Cities***

"Behind him, across vast distances of space and time, from the place he had left, he thought he heard music too. But perhaps it was only an echo."

—***The Giver***

"And they walked away together through the hole in the wall, back into the darkness, leaving nothing behind them; not even the doorway."

—***Neverwhere***

Q: Why did women shave their legs in the Middle Ages? A: To get rid of fleas and lice.

THE LAST PAGE

FELLOW BATHROOM READERS:

Bathroom reading should never be taken loosely, so Sit Down and Be Counted! Log on to *www.bathroomreader.com* and earn a permanent spot on the BRI honor roll! And while you're there...

- Visit "The Throne Room"—a great place to read!
- Receive our irregular newsletters via e-mail
- Order additional *Bathroom Readers*
- Face us on Facebook
- Tweet us on Twitter
- Blog us on our blog

UNCLE JOHN'S NEXT *BATHROOM READER FOR KIDS ONLY* IS ALREADY IN THE WORKS!

Is there a subject you'd like to see in our next *Uncle John's Bathroom Reader* for kids? Write to us at www.bathroomreader.com and let us know. We aim to please.

Well, we're out of space, and when you've got to go, you've got to go. Hope to hear from you soon. Meanwhile, remember...

Go with the Flow!